The Key to Triumphant Living

*TO WHOM GOD WOULD MAKE KNOWN
WHAT IS THE RICHES OF THE GLORY OF
THIS MYSTERY AMONG THE GENTILES;
WHICH IS CHRIST IN YOU, THE HOPE OF
GLORY.*
Colossians 1:27

THE KEY TO TRIUMPHANT LIVING

BROADMAN PRESS
Nashville, Tennessee

Library of Congress Catalog Card Number: 76–166582
Dewey Decimal Classification: 248.4
Subject Heading: CHRISTIAN LIFE
Printed in the United States of America

<u>DEDICATION</u>

To the glory of God, the exaltation of Christ, and the
honor of the Holy Spirit . . .

To my little family . . . Barbara, Tammy, and Timmy
on earth, and Terry in heaven . . .

To my previous church, the Castle Hills First Baptist
Church, San Antonio, Texas . . .

To the prayer groups who bathed every moment of the
work on this volume in fervent intercession . . .

To Pauline Burrows and Gail Webb for work on the
manuscript . . .

To everyone, everywhere, who is looking for the KEY
TO TRIUMPHANT LIVING . . .

I prayerfully present this volume.

JACK R. TAYLOR

THOUGHTS ABOUT
THE KEY TO TRIUMPHANT LIVING

There are several reasons why it thrills my heart to write about this volume.

First, I sense a hunger in the hearts of the Lord's people over our land for a triumphant life of usefulness to the Lord in contrast to their laborious toil of good works done in the energy of the flesh.

Second, I believe that those who are now enjoying abundant life in Christ's enthronement will be refreshed and stimulated by the message of this book.

Third, I am excited over the extent to which this book has been used and is being used.

Fourth, I am excited because this book is more than doctrine. It throbs with the joy of victories freshly given because the author writes it from a life of overflowing. The Lord has richly used his preaching and teaching of the Word across the land . . . and around the world.

Finally, I am thrilled to believe that readers of this book will experience such great conviction of sins, such brokenness over their sinful natures, such deep desires to be cleansed and Christ-possessed that they will be moved to meet God's requirements and become the Lord's empowered witnesses.

BERTHA SMITH

After eighteen years in the Christian life, and while pastor of his second pastorate in Texas, the Castle Hills First Baptist Church of San Antonio, Jack Taylor came to his wit's end, and in a little upper room in Houston in 1964, there was an unemotional experience but a life-changing experience! He learned that he was "never meant to be something but contain Someone, and that Someone is Jesus."

A mutual friend said: "Jack Taylor is doing for us spiritually what a popcorn machine does for our physical appetites; he is causing a spiritual hunger!" And yet this is not Jack Taylor's "doings" but the Lord who lives in Jack Taylor doing it through him!

EULA MAE HENDERSON

I have literally been swept away by the "Divine Flow" of which this book speaks. Overpowering periods in which I have known confession of sins, a deepening of my prayer life, and an exploding awareness of His sweet, majestic Presence have done more for my own life in a handful of weeks than I have known in a lifetime of ministry.

It is my earnest prayer that the reader of this volume will not approach it as a theological treatise to be reviewed. It does not contain a *theology,* but an *experience* which has, and does, change a baby Christian into a mature, Christ-filled earthen vessel. May His Holy Spirit give each reader this important truth of the Spirit-filled life as an *experience,* not a *concept.*

RALPH W. NEIGHBOUR, JR.

<u>CONTENTS</u>

INTRODUCTION

This is not a theological treatise but a study adventure in personal discovery. It is the story of people who, within the context of *despair,* came upon a vital *discovery* which opened the way to a life of *delight.* On my part it is an experience so thoroughly fulfilling that I have kept waiting to write a full report of it in the past tense. I realize now that this is impossible since the experience is ever continuing and Jesus is always saving the best for *now!* The subject matter of this book is simply Jesus Christ indwelling the believer by his Holy Spirit. Of necessity the discussion will lead to a study of the believer's relationship with the Holy Spirit, who magnifies Christ and fills the believer with Christ-life.

The key, in a statement, is CHRIST IN YOU . . . THE HOPE OF GLORY. It is by the Holy Spirit that Christ *comes to live* in the human spirit, *abides to master* the human spirit, and *continues to minister* through the human spirit to a world in desperate need.

There is much emphasis today on the need of a new dynamic. A trumpet sounds out a new possibility or a new power and thousands are ready and eager to listen. There are uncertain sounds in the area of renewal which bypass or disregard the ministry of the Holy Spirit. These sounds are destined to die out among the howling winds of human need.

"Honor the Holy Ghost!" was the plea of an old man to Dwight L. Moody in the beginning days of his evangelistic ministry. He never forgot that admonition. That movement or person which does not honor the Spirit cannot succeed. Those who honestly, scripturally, and sanely honor the Holy Spirit as he magnifies Christ cannot fail.

The subject matter of this volume is not new. It is as old as the Scripture. But we are experiencing in these troubled times a ground swell of interest in the ministry of the Holy Spirit. With such interest the executive offices of hell are buzzing with business. New attacks from the adversary are being mobilized against God's people. Confusion abounds. Clear notes need to characterize the trumpets which sound today. I pray that this work will be a clear sound. It is simple and so intended. It is the simple story of how a simple principle brought simple people to the end of self, to discover the beginning of a new life in a sufficient Savior.

HE IS THE KEY . . . .

    LIVING IN ME . . . .

        BY THE HOLY SPIRIT!

There are many ways to say it:

Hannah W. Smith calls it THE CHRISTIAN'S
    SECRET TO A HAPPY LIFE;

    Charles Trumbull, VICTORY IN CHRIST;

        Ian Thomas, THE SAVING LIFE OF CHRIST;

            Stuart Briscoe, THE FULNESS OF CHRIST;

                A. B. Simpson, THE LARGER LIFE;

                    Harold Wildish, THE GLORIOUS
                        SECRET;

                        F. B. Meyer, THE EXCHANGED
                            LIFE;

G. B. Duncan titles it THE LIFE OF CONTINUAL
REJOICING:

Watchman Nee, THE NORMAL CHRISTIAN
LIFE;

Ruth Paxson, LIFE ON THE HIGHEST
PLANE;

and still others such as Huegel, Barbour, Maxwell,
McConkey, Redpath, Hunter, Tryon, Murray, Finney,
and Letgers have varying terms for what Jesus simply
called LIFE MORE ABUNDANT!

This quality of life has been appropriately called the
Spirit-controlled life, the Christ-filled life, the overcoming
life, life in the heavenlies, and the key to everything.

Whatever it is called, it is nothing less than all of
Christ . . .

resident in. . . .

reigning over. . . .

and released through

the human life. This is the master key. This is the KEY
TO TRIUMPHANT LIVING. I do not know of a lock
it doesn't fit.

It is toward the reader's knowing with the mind and
experiencing with the life of this open secret that this
book is written. May the reading of it be an unforgettable
experience with the living Lord through his Spirit, and
may it be the means by which God is able to begin revival
where you are!

JACK R. TAYLOR

PART I
THE *RESIDENCE* OF CHRIST *IN* THE HUMAN LIFE

"Christ in you, the hope of glory"
Colossians 1:27*b*

"CHRIST IS LIVING IN ME . . ."
Galatians 2:20

"Shall I tell you why my life now is so easy?
'Tis because this wretched self has ceased to be;
Once it caused me all my troubles, but it's buried,
And it is no longer I, BUT CHRIST IN ME."
A. B. Simpson

PART I
WIT'S END

"At their wit's end . . . they cry unto the Lord in their trouble, and he BRINGETH THEM OUT" (Ps. 107:27,28).

Wit's end! That was my permanent address for a number of years! I wasn't alone, but that didn't help much. My neighbors were intolerable. Next door was Jealousy; across the street, Mr. Competition; and down the way, the Despair family. Old Man Politics haunted me by promising me much and delivering nothing but worry. I suppose I made an honest effort to move out of the neighborhood. But each effort ended in frustration. So it seemed that the discreet thing to do was to settle down in a rather quiet but well-rationalized despair and fake it as best I could.

There was one enormous problem. I was paid to tell people at wit's end how to get out. I was a preacher. I was supposed to have all the answers. I didn't even have the right questions! This makes the preacher's job something which should be marked with the warning "CAUTION: THIS MAY BE HAZARDOUS TO YOUR SANITY."

I learned something about the neighborhood of Wit's End. If you live in the last house there is no place to go but up.

Are you standing at "Wit's End Corner,"
Christian, with troubled brow?

Are you thinking of what is before you,
>   And all you are bearing now?
Does all the world seem against you,
>   And you in the battle alone?"
Remember . . . at "wit's end corner"
>   Is just where God's power is shown![1]

The story you are about to hear is true. The names
and places have been unchanged to expose the guilty.
Do not be surprised if at intervals you stop and say,
"Hey, he's telling MY story." I am convinced that it is
the story of most lives somewhere within the context of
the Christian walk. If I could have chosen a longer title
for this chapter, it would have been "HOW I MOVED
FROM WIT'S END LANE TO PRAISE THE LORD
BOULEVARD!" This is my story. Forgive the inevitable
personal references and the detail. Be assured that they
are there with a design in mind. Happy reading!

I received Christ into my life when I was ten years
old. After the typical instruction afforded by my church
in the Christian life, I embarked upon the sea of Christian
adventure. (The instruction was, "Please sit down!") I
do not remember anybody ever telling me what had happened to me when I was saved. There I was, all dressed
up in a new experience and nowhere to go.

MISLEARNING BY DEDUCTION

My father was a farmer and a very good one. I suppose
that I simply deduced that if my father could become a
good farmer by hard work, I could become a good Christian in the same manner. I do not ever remember not
wanting to be a good Christian. So I set out *trying* to
be what I had become. A sandy-land farm is not exactly
the shortest route to becoming a millionaire, but my dad

made it do. He had a few washouts, blowouts, hail-outs, some straight out crop failures, and every now and then a fair crop. So I figured that this was what I would have to settle for in the Christian life. Thus, for almost two decades, my Christian life was like that of a sharecropper on a sandy-land farm. I tolerated it simply because I didn't know there was anything else. Nobody ever told me what the Christian life was all about.

CALLED TO PREACH

I didn't surrender to preach. When I found out God was calling me, I jumped at the chance! I began preaching at fourteen and despite the terrible inferiority complex that was to plague me for the next several years I discovered a measure of joy in preaching. I went to college at sixteen to "learn how to be a preacher." I always had the feeling that somewhere in this Christian life there had to be more. This just couldn't be all there was! I held on by the simple belief that somewhere at sometime I would wake up a howling success and discover what I had been looking for in complete fulfilment. Again, with the principle I learned on the farm, I worked hard. Hard work brought its attendant rewards but not the missing ingredient I had sought. I kept thinking that around the next sermon, the next revival, the next prayer meeting, or the next "A" in Social Ethics, there victory would be staring me in the face. It simply didn't happen.

THE HOLY SPIRIT . . . DISMISSED

My grandparents were members of a religious group whose emotional extremes and physical distortions made up the best entertainment in our little town. Thus, when it was suggested that what I really needed was to be filled with the Holy Spirit, I politely said, "No, thank you!" You see, when I thought of being filled with the Spirit, my mind went back to those cavortings I watched with amusement under the brush arbor next to the church on the hill. It was as simple as this . . . I dismissed the fact that the Holy Spirit could be the source of the fulfilment I needed. (I was later to change my mind.)

A CHANCE TO SUCCEED

After pastoring a grand little rural church where people were so kind to me in my ignorance, I moved to the suburbs of this thriving metropolis to the pastorate of a church whose membership was a little more than one hundred. I had three advantages:

> I meant well,
> > I was willing to work,
> > > and

I wanted more than anything else in life to succeed! Now, keep in mind, nobody yet (that I could remember) ever stopped me to tell me about the great secrets of the Christian life. So I simply worked hard, prayed much, did the best I could, and rededicated my life every now and then just for good measure. I must admit to you now (though I wouldn't have then) that it was pretty miserable trying to outwit the critical and outwork the witty.

But, alas, hard work began to pay off. God has to use what he can get, so he used us. I am now convinced that most of what he did that was allowed to stand, he had to do despite me and not because of me. There was success. In fact, after five years, I had a chance to prove that success did not hold the discovery of that secret I longed for more than anything else in the world.

I woke up one day at twenty-nine years of age with everything my system had taught me to have ambition for, and I was MISERABLE!

SICK AND TIRED

That was it . . . I WAS SICK AND TIRED OF BE-ING SICK AND TIRED! My misery, accumulated over the years, began to worsen. I prayed more and worked harder. I caught myself sacrificing my wonderful family, Barbara, Tammy, and Timmy, on the altar of ministerial success. Frantically evading self-discovery, I sought more success in *buildings, budgets,* and *baptisms,* too often our "holy trinity" of success. Nothing seemed to lessen the miseries, depression, and pressures. I wanted out but there seemed no way. My only relief was in those islands of rationalization when my confidence was bolstered by success. But God was laying hold of me! I couldn't outrun him! At last I was in such anguish that I prayed to die. I did that frequently and over a period of several weeks. During that time my disillusionment became almost un-bearable. I knew that it would not be long before I left the ministry or cracked up or both!

Doubt, depression, discouragement, and despair were my constant companions. Undoubtedly I was at "wit's end corner."

> Are you standing at "Wit's End Corner"?
>   Then you're just in the very spot
> To learn the wondrous resources
>   Of him who faileth not.
> No doubt to a brighter pathway
>   Your footsteps will soon be moved,
> But only at "Wit's End Corner"
>   Is the "God who is able" proved.[2]

And that was what was about to happen!

THE BEGINNING OF A TURN

I remember one night praying a prayer something like this, "Lord, I have prayed again and again that you would take my life. I don't know why you have not answered my prayer. I am going to pray one more time, and if you let me wake up in the morning, I am going to take it from you as a promise that there is indeed something more in the Christian life than what I have found." I went to bed not caring whether I ever awakened or not.

The obvious fact is that I did wake up. One of the first conscious thoughts that I had was this, "All right, Lord, I accept the fact that I am alive this morning as your promise that there is something more. I thank you for whatever it is."

I remember going to the Bible, the book I had never doubted. I just knew that whatever answer there was must be in the Book. I had thumbed its pages many times looking for what it had to say to others. I now went to it as a beggar in search of bread. There was too much talk in the Bible about victory, overcoming, abundant life, and continuous joy for me to settle for an existence like I had. I was desperate, depressed, disillusioned, discouraged, disgusted, and deeply desirous for God to do something he had never done before in me. I was ready for that moment:

> I wish there was some wonderful place,
>   Called the Land of Beginning Again
> Where all our mistakes, and all our heartaches,
>   And all of our selfish griefs,
> Could be cast like a shabby old coat at the door
>   And never be put on again!

"The Land of Beginning Again." I thought of the words which formed the title of one of my favorite sermons. I had preached it often. Now I needed to hear it more than anybody! A hungry heart stirred anxious hands to search the Scriptures. The first place I remember reading was the first chapter of the book of Colossians. The mystery of it intrigued me. Paul spoke of a *mystery* that had been hidden from ages and generations and now was made known to all the saints. I read with increasing anticipation as if I had never read the book before, feeling myself to be on the verge of an exciting discovery. (Little did I know what a discovery it would be!)

Then I came across it! "TO WHOM GOD WOULD MAKE KNOWN WHAT IS THE RICHES OF THE GLORY OF THIS MYSTERY AMONG THE GENTILES; WHICH IS

CHRIST IN YOU, THE HOPE OF GLORY" (Col. 1:27). I wish I could convey to you what went on in my mind the moment those words began to sink into my poor soul! Some day God is going to give me the benefit of an instant replay of that moment and many other moments since then that I do not have words to describe.

A REVERSING REVELATION

CHRIST LIVES IN ME! He is real and vital and alive in me! I saw it; I felt it; and I knew it! He had been there all the time, watching, longing, and waiting to be my new life. I was too busy trying to be like him, trying to serve him, and trying to promote him. Now, I knew that what really happened that day almost twenty years before was that Jesus, himself, really came to live his life in me. What I had done because of ignorance was to put Christ in a corner and steal an occasional glance at him and say, "I am going to be like you if it kills me!" It almost had. Now the shattering realization was mine that I had for those years worked *against* God's arrangement for my life. His purpose was that Christ should come and find in my life a willing instrument, a means of transportation and expression for his very own life. I had busied myself in trying to be like him and trying to do his work in such a way as to disallow his work in me! I had prevented the very thing I desired more than anything in life.

CHRIST LIVES IN ME! What a lovely, lifting, liberating thought that was. I had read that verse before. In fact, it had been the text for a sermon that I had preached. But those words that followed never had grabbed my attention, "THE HOPE OF GLORY!" "The" is a very exclusive word. I had found hope in earthly pleasures, successful work, ministerial attainment, and material possessions. For the first time I looked at both those facts together—

CHRIST IS IN ME . . .
THAT IS *THE* HOPE OF GLORY!

The hope of my ever being what I was made to become is that Christ lives in me to assure it and achieve it!

I lived in the next months in gleeful delight of a new discovery. I was busy in the Book as if it were a new book. Whole chapters came alive that were obscure before. Jesus became somebody real that walked out of its pages and fellowshiped with me. I fell in love anew with this wonderful Somebody named Jesus. I began to feel like a child excited over Christmas. The only difference was that it was *every* day.

In those days there were waves of revelations coming over me as I read the Bible and other literature with ravenous appetite. I gave myself to the pursuit of God. He graciously guided me to this experience and that, to this author and that, to this chapter and that in the Book. I began to put fact upon fact and delight was added to delight.

All Of God Was In Christ . . .
   All Of Christ Was In Me . . .
All I Needed Was Christ Himself . . .
   And I Had Him Living Inside Me!

But then I began to realize that just *to know* was not enough. As glorious as the revelation was that Christ was alive in me, it was obvious that my life was still subject to little besetting sins. My emotions still moved up and down like a roller coaster. My victory was intermittent. It's not enough just to know!

REVELATION BECOMES EXPERIENTIAL

The language of this new life was beautiful. I used it freely. A preacher who was a stranger to me asked me to preach a revival in his church in Houston, Texas. The basis on which he asked me was my knowledge of the life in Christ. Little did he know how little I knew! The big crisis came in that meeting. I came face to face with the realization that I was not above taking the beautiful message of the indwelling Christ and using it to my advantage in selfish advancement. I saw myself: a hypocrite, capable of anything, regardless of its nature, against God. I admitted to God that I was a scheming, conniving, maneuvering, egotistical fraud! I confessed every known sin in my life. I suppose I waited for the heavens to reply in awe, surprise, and disappointment. Instead, I got the overwhelming impression that God had been "on to me" all along. It was as if he said, "I have been waiting for you to find that out. Now, since you have, why don't we let my original arrangement come to pass? You see, when I saved you, Jesus himself came to live in you! It's Jesus, only, that you need to live the life I require and you desire." God still loved me even though he knew what I was like! Then I was free to accept his acceptance of me.

It was on that night, over twenty years after I had received Christ into my heart as Savior, that I wholly and heartily yielded myself to him as unconditional Lord of my life. I asked him to reign without a rival from then on in my life. I said, "Jesus, I want you to get on the throne of my life and never get off again. I sign a contract with you tonight, releasing all rights to myself and my life. Put me where you will, doing what you will, as you will. I give up to you. I am through! Begin your public ministry through me right now!"

There were no bright lights, no voices, and very little emotion. There *was* an overwhelming and awesome certainty that a transaction between Christ and me had been validated. I wasn't sure just what had happened. I didn't have the language to describe it. I didn't even know exactly what to call it. Terms were not so important to me then. Reality was the beautiful thing. The struggle was over. Rest came. Joy was spontaneous. The liberty was fantastic . . .

> free from trying and futile struggle . . .
> free from the prison of statistics . . .
> free from the demand to succeed at any price. . .
> *free! free!*

I was free to fail in all human appearances if that's what success is to God. I was free to follow Christ without thoughts as to the personal outcome. I was free from having to engage in "amateur providence," that cheap maneuvering we are often given to under the guise of piety. I was free from having to prove myself to myself and to others. I was free from having to be constantly conscious of self, always worried about how "it" was going to come out for me.

By the way, did I tell you that in the process of it all I lost that horrid *inferiority complex?* Yes, I lost it! It dissolved in a simple discovery—I WAS JUST PLAIN INFERIOR! The fact was faced. The complex was gone. But I had the Christ of God living in me!

THREE PRAYERS GOD DID NOT FORGET

Before I leave that night in Houston, I want to share with you three prayers that the Holy Spirit voiced through me. First, I prayed that I would never go back from what had happened to me. I prayed that God would never let me turn around and go back to the life that I had once known. I even went so far as to pray that if I ever prayed a prayer contrary to the one I was praying then, he wouldn't answer it. That locked me in! How many times has he reminded me of that prayer! Praise the Lord, he hasn't let me go back. For seven wonderful years I have felt pleasingly pushed along on the path of abundant life!

Second, I prayed that I would see this happen to the lives of those around me. (I still didn't know what to call what had happened.) I had felt so all alone in my despair. Now I felt all alone in my delight and wanted desperately someone with whom to share my testimony. You, my dear reader, are one of the thousands of answers to this prayer.

Third, I prayed that God would use me in the life of my denomination. I loved it, and yet it was within the context of its system that I had missed the central dynamic of the Christian faith. I had succeeded in all the ways it had taught me to want to succeed, and yet I had not made the *vital discovery* of CHRIST LIVING IN ME! How wonderful has been God's continuing answer to this prayer he prayed through me! This book itself is a part of the accumulated answer to that prayer. I pray that just a fraction of the excitement I am feeling as I write it will be sensed by the reader as he or she moves through it.

THE EXPERIENCE IN RETROSPECT

What really happened that night in Houston? Whatever it was is still happening. I always stop myself when I try to tell of the experience in the past tense. Some suggest that surely I was saved that night and just thought I had been saved before. I have had seven years to think about it. All of Webster's words cannot form a descriptive network around it. It was like being saved all over again. This I will admit. But I had trusted Christ as my personal Savior when I was ten. I can share with you now from the deepest convictions of my heart that this is what happened:

The Holy Spirit, against whom I was unknowingly prejudiced by unfortunate past exposures, had been faithful to do his work in me. He had convicted me and had brought me to self-discovery and thus to despair. He had made Christ beautiful and real. I gladly chose against myself in preference to Christ. I invited him to the throne of my life! He became my Lord. In that fantastic experience . . . HE HAD FILLED ME WITH HIS HOLY SPIRIT! I had found the *KEY!* The Holy Spirit had done his work in spite of my ignorance through the glorious concept of the indwelling Christ. Since then I have happily realized that it was all brought about by the Holy Spirit. It was through his Spirit that I was indwelt of the Savior. It was through his Spirit that I was being led along in the knowledge of him. It was through his Spirit that he filled me with himself.

The day that I honored the blessed Holy Spirit by acknowledging him as the One who did it all, a new wave of glory broke over my soul. I wept and laughed as "joy unspeakable and full of glory" surged through my heart.

In the years that have followed, how wonderful that key has become! If the discovery itself was wonderful, how multiplied the wonder as I discovered that key to fit every lock around me barring the way to abundant life. Doors, long since closed, are flung open.

I have seen the key open the lock of . . .
PERSONAL DISILLUSIONMENT . . .
MARITAL DISHARMONY . . .
SELF CONDEMNATION . . .
FEAR . . .
ANXIETY . . .
DEPRESSION . . .
AND FLING OPEN THE DOOR UPON A NEW AND WONDERFUL LIFE!

It came, I know not how,
But this I know, that now
My life has found a new and nobler plane,
Something old has passed away,
Something new has come to stay.
And I can never be the same again.

The Change is not in me.
Rather, it seems that he
Has come himself to live his life in mine
And as I stepped aside,

And took him to abide . . .
He came and filled me with his life divine.

The key to triumphant living is simply . . .
　　Christ in me . . . Christ in you . . .
　　　The hope of glory!

Wit's End Lane is no longer my address. Mark the
　　change of address . . .
　　　Jack Taylor
　　　Praise the Lord Boulevard
　　　　It's Glorious!
　　　　Praise the Lord!

PART I
AN EXAMPLE WE DARE NOT IGNORE

"Now these things were our examples, to the intent
we should not lust after evil things, as they also lusted
. . . and they are written for our admonition, upon whom
the ends of the world are come" (1 Cor. 10:6,11).

They came to the gates of Canaan,
But they never entered in;
They came to the very threshold,
But they perished in their sin.

And so we are ever coming
To the place where two ways part,
One leads to the land of promise,
And one to a hardened heart.

One of the most valid sources of truth for the Christian
is to be found in the history of the Israelites from Egypt

to Canaan. We dare not ignore this vast storehouse of spiritual truth. It is more than just history. It typifies every stage of the life of the children of God in every age.

Israel in Egypt is a picture of where we were when the Lord found us in our sins. Egypt symbolizes the world, according to the course of which we walked. There we see the tyranny of sin and the hate of the adversary. The misery of the children of God reflects the groanings of a soul under conviction of sin.

In Moses is the type of our Deliverer, Jesus Christ the Messiah. The Red Sea experience reflects our salvation experience where we cross over from one life to another. The previous Passover night tells of the believers' security under the redeeming blood of the cross.

There is the wilderness wandering affording us a picture of the spiritual pilgrimage of God's children today. The tabernacle is a graduate course in the excellencies and glories of the Savior. Its fittings and furnishings show us his majesty like a bright jewel held up in the sun.

Every stage of the journey of Israel is freighted with lessons of spiritual significance. There are types of Christ all along the way. There is Moses, the deliverer. Then we see the smitten rock out of which gushed the water of supply. Later on we observe Joshua "bringing them in," symbolizing the other ministry of Jesus. Many have allowed Jesus to "take them out" of spiritual Egypt, but few have allowed him to "take them in" to spiritual Canaan.

For those seeking the key to triumphant living, the example of the children of Israel is priceless. The significance of our brief observation of this panorama of spiritual truth will be found in discovering just where we are individually in our personal spiritual pilgrimage. This will position us to continue our study with proper perspective.

Every person living in the world today is in one of three places spiritually speaking . . . Egypt, the Wilderness, or Canaan. Let us observe the characteristics of these places spiritually.

EGYPT

We have briefly stated already that Egypt paints a vivid picture of the one who walks according to the course of this world. It is the picture of the *natural* man, his nature, his plight, and his hopelessness. He is lost as a result of his wilful choice to disobey God. He is enslaved to labor without purpose, as is any man today who walks without Christ. Let's look at this *natural* man a little more closely through the eyes of Paul in 1 Corinthians, chapter 2. First, he is bound to the material world. "The natural man receiveth not the things of the spirit . . ." (1 Cor. 2:14). Thus, second, he is blind to the spiritual. Third, he is cut off from his inheritance and simply does not have the Spirit of God living in him.

THE WILDERNESS

This phase of the journey of the children of Israel was not meant to be permanent. There is a time in every Christian's life which can be recognized as "wilderness wandering," but it was intended to be a time of spiritual learning before the blessed "Canaan experience." One writer suggests that this is the "legitimate" wilderness experience. It is that time when the new Christian comes against the problems he will be facing all along his life and learns of God's wonderful resources. The hardships of the wilderness prepare the new saint for the warfare in Canaan. But there is the "illegitimate" wilderness experience which always comes after the cries of Kadesh-Bar-

THE KEY TO TRIUMPHANT LIVING

nea. The Christian refuses full surrender and turns from Canaan's victory. He walks back into the wilderness into living death. This is the picture of many thousands of Christians today who have "come out" but have not "come in." They have forgotten that just as it was with the Israelites, so with them. "And he brought us out from thence, that he might bring us in, to give us the land which he sware unto out fathers" (Deut. 6:23).

This illegitimate wilderness gives us a picture of the most common kind of Christian today, the *carnal* Christian. He is saved from *sin* but not saved from *self.* He ranges all the time somewhere between the Egypt side of the wilderness and the Canaan side. He has had a chance to "go in" but has found it too risky. He is restless and fruitless, unstable and negative. He vacillates between the two borders of Egypt and Canaan. Ruth Paxson characterizes the carnal Christian in this manner:

He has a life of unceasing conflict . . .
  Of repeated defeat,
    Of protracted infancy,
      Of barren fruitlessness,
        Of adulterous infidelity . . . and
        Of dishonoring hypocrisy.

Romans 7 is his permanent address. Frustration abounds. Futility reigns. Such is the life of a Christian in the wilderness. Are you here? You don't have to stay. There is something better. That is what this book is about! Let us go on to . . .

CANAAN

We often make the mistake of making Canaan the symbol of heaven later on instead of Christian victory here and now. This mistake has led many a person to accept

32 JACK R. TAYLOR

a life of quiet despair without knowing of the "much more" of the Christ life. The spiritual significance of Canaan is doubtless the picture of the life of victory afforded by the indwelling Christ *this side of* heaven. It is a beautiful painting of the Spirit-filled life with its battles and victories.

Canaan stands for the "heavenly places" Paul refers to in Ephesians and for the "much more" he speaks of in Romans 5. It is the life of continual rejoicing depicted in Philippians. Canaan is the land of triumphant living which belongs to every Christian who has discovered the key . . . *Christ in you,* the hope of glory! Let's look a little more closely at this citizen of Canaan. He is *educated* in the things of God. "That we might know the things that are freely given to us of God" (1 Cor. 2:12). He is *expressive* of spiritual values. "Which things also we speak, not in words which man's wisdom teacheth, but which the Holy Ghost teacheth; comparing spiritual things with spiritual" (1 Cor. 2:13). *He evaluates* spiritual things. "He that is spiritual judgeth all things . . ." (1 Cor. 2:15). The life of this "Canaan man" is an enigma to the world. His appetites and ambitions are otherwordly. He is a citizen of heaven and a stranger to this world. Ruth Paxson describes him thusly:

> He has a life of abiding peace,
>   of habitual victory,
>   of constant growth in Christlikeness,
>   of supernatural power,
>   of devoted separateness and
>   of winsome holiness.

So in spiritual geography we have three distinct places. Every reader is in one of these right now! Where are you? Are you in Egypt? Then linger no longer. Come to Jesus now and enjoy your pilgrimage to Canaan's plenty. Are you in the wilderness? Are you discouraged, defeated, and despairing? The following chapters are for you! Are you in Canaan? Praise the Lord! Isn't it glorious? But on beyond there is more. We can continue to experience the victory as we "possess our possessions."

This mini-chapter will serve to help you know where you are in the pilgrimage of life. Come with me as we discover THE KEY TO TRIUMPHANT LIVING. He who "brought us out" is on hand to "bring us in."

PART 1
THE ENEMY THAT BLOCKS OUR PATH

"O wretched man that I am! who shall deliver me from the body of this death?" (Rom. 7:24).

> There is a foe whose hidden power
>   The Christian well may fear,
> More subtle far than inbred sin,
>   And to the heart more dear.
>
> It is the power of selfishness,
>   It is the wilful "I",
> And ere my Lord can live in me,
>   My very self must die.[3]

Go ahead and admit it! You are your greatest problem. You are your chief enemy. Of all the four-letter words, SELF is the worst. If you can just face it and acknowledge it, you will be one step closer to victory. Before we can properly observe the glories of the Christ-indwelt life, we must come face to face with this enemy who would occupy the throne of our lives and ever keep us from triumph.

THE CHOICE OF SELF

Let's go back to the time when the enemy first appeared. God made man and placed him in a very beautiful and completely self-contained paradise. He walked with man and enjoyed his company. He had made man for fellowship, but to be valid, man had to choose to fellowship with God. If there was choice, of necessity, there had to be an alternative. Thus, the Bible tells us that there was a tree in the midst of the garden called the *tree of life.* Man was free to eat of it and of any other tree in his paradise. They were made for his happiness and supply. That tree of life was to be the means by which man could live on and on. If man's choice to eat of the tree called Life was to be valid, there had to be an alternative. Thus, in the "midst of the garden" (the same place as the tree called Life) was another tree, *the tree of knowledge of good and evil.* It represented to man his independent right to choose against God if he wished. This was the only manner in which man's choice to love and serve Jehovah God would be valid. If he chose to eat of the tree of life he would never know the difference between good and evil because he would not *need* to. He would ever be taking of the fruit of the tree of life, the life of God, and he would always be good as God is good. He would always be living in utter dependence on God.

But man chose the tree of knowledge of good and evil. He would rather develop his life as he saw fit and "do his own thing." He would be self-sufficient and independent.

Self took the throne.
    God was shoved aside.
        Man fell and with his fall
creation was thrown into imbalance and chaos.

Man's great enemy was SELF. He had made the choice. Sin would now reign unto death. The path to the tree of life was blocked, and man was cast out of the garden. He had chosen his own way, and he must now bear the consequences. We bear in our lives now the result of those consequences. The choice has been ours that was Adam's. We have chosen between the tree of life and the tree of knowledge of good and evil. The fruit of the first tree is Christ. The fruit of the second tree is self. We are always making a choice between the two.

THE CHARACTER OF SELF

Satan embodies the character of self. It was because he made the big "I" his pivot that he became the devil. Listen to Isaiah's quote of Lucifer: "For thou has said in thine heart, I will ascend into heaven, I will exalt my throne above the stars of God: I will sit also upon the mount of the congregation, in the sides of the north: I will ascend above the heights of the clouds; I will be like the most High" (Isa. 14:13-14). Satan had "I" trouble.

When man did what Satan wanted him to do, he became infected with the same disease of SELF. He then possessed a nature incorrigible to God. Self became the archenemy. Another word for self is the "flesh." This is what we are without Christ. "They that are in the flesh [self] cannot please God" (Rom. 8:8).

Self is not subject to the law of God, nor can it ever be. "Because the carnal mind is enmity against God: for it is not subject to the law of God neither indeed can be" (Rom 8:7). Self cannot be *domesticated*. This is a vital point which kept me from victory for many years. I thought surely that something must have happened to my "self" nature when I got saved. Years after my conversion I heard a preacher say that nothing happened to that self when I got saved, absolutely nothing. It didn't improve one iota! Now, isn't that shocking? Christ didn't come in to improve self but to replace it. Self has no place in the economy of God.

Neither can you discipline it. How busy we are trying to discipline self. But it is hopelessly incorrigible. It is wild and deceitful. You can educate it, change its living conditions, and expose it to the highest kind of morality, but self is still "deceitful above all things and desperately wicked." There is no "good" self and "bad" self as far as God is concerned. The self-life represents everything foreign to the nature of God. Wherever its nature is manifest, there is "adultery, fornication, uncleanness, lasciviousness, idolatry, witchcraft, hatred, variance, emulations, wrath, strife, seditions, heresies, envyings, murders, drunkenness, revellings, and such like" (Gal. 5:19-21).

Self must not be *dedicated.* How prone we are to try to do that! The accumulated result of the effort to dedicate self is a system that operates on selfish motivation and selfish rewards. We have in our church acres and acres of dedicated self (which is not dedication at all). Self will do anything before it will die. It will pray, work, and tithe. It will teach a Sunday School class or become a deacon. It will even preach! It will steep itself in religious tradition to cushion itself against God. But it remains an enemy of God. As long as self and Christ remain in the same heart there will be war.

THE COURSE OF SELF

Self is committed to an unchanging course of godlessness. It will *defeat* us. Listen to Paul as he cries: "For I know that in me (that is, in my flesh,) dwelleth no good thing: for to will is present with me; but how to perform that which is good I find not. For the good that

I would I do not: but the evil which I would not, that I do. For I delight in the law of God after the inward man: But I see another law in my members, warring against the law of my mind, and *bringing me into captivity* to the law of sin which is in my members" (Rom. 7:18-19, 22-23). It will *despair* us. There is no greater cry of despair than that of Paul in Romans 7:24, "O wretched man that I am! who shall deliver me from the body of this death?" It will *doom* us. Its summary consequence is simply stated in Romans 8:6, "For to be carnally minded is DEATH."

The course of self is pre-plotted. It will look at everything with an eye as to how it will be affected. It will always magnify itself. It is touchy, sensitive when not recognized, and always struggles for the position of highest honor and praise. It cannot bear to be rebuked or corrected. It is full of self-defense. It pushes its claims and petty notions on other people. It is destructive and deadly.

> Oh, to be saved from myself, dear Lord!
> Oh, to be lost in thee!
> Oh, that it might be no more I,
> But Christ that lives in me!

Well, if you can't domesticate it or discipline it or dedicate it, what can you do with it? If its course is changeless, what can be done? Are you ready to give up on all your methods of handling self? If you are, we are ready to go to God's method.

THE CURE OF SELF

In a tree there is a type of vascular tissue called the xylem. This type of cell is used to bring minerals and water, the life-giving substance of a tree, to the various parts of the tree from the ground.

The unique thing about these cells is that they are of no use to the tree until they are dead. In a living cell there is cytoplasm and the nucleus, which is the cell nature. As long as this nature lives, it blocks the flow of life-giving substances that are so desperately needed by the tree.

Likewise the Christian is of no use to God until he is dead. He cannot live completely to the God nature as long as he continues to live to his own nature.

There is but one cure for self . . . DEATH! Death is the only means of deliverance from the self-life. We cannot kill ourselves nor does God intend it. He does intend that we accept the full implication of the death of Jesus. If he died for us, then we died. If we died, then we are no longer alive. We are then to "reckon" ourselves to be dead to sin and alive to God through Christ. We are not called to a process of self-crucifixion but to the acceptance of a crucifixion already accomplished. Paul said, "I am crucified with Christ: nevertheless I live; yet not I, but Christ liveth in me" (Gal. 2:20). Then we can shout:

> I am crucified with Jesus,
> > And the cross has set me free;
> I have risen again with Jesus,
> > And he lives and reigns in me!
> It is sweet to die with Jesus,
> > To the world, and self, and sin.
> It is sweet to live with Jesus
> > As he lives and reigns within.[4]

The cure of self is death. Jesus Christ alone offers this cure. He said, "If any man will come after me, let him deny himself, and take up his cross daily, and follow me" (Luke 9:23). Such a proposition deserves closer investigation. Let us draw some facts from that statement:

It is possible to follow Jesus. He invites it. But there are rigid qualifications. One must choose against himself. Further, one must take up his cross daily. What could this mean? It simply means that if I am to follow Christ, I must accept the fact of my death and keep on accepting it. If Jesus were speaking today, he would use whatever means of death that was acceptable in that locale. In one state it would be the *gallows,* in another the *gas chamber,* in still another the *electric chair.* These add up to only one thing . . . *death.* If I am to follow Christ, I must figuratively sit down in that chair of execution. I must wilfully tighten the belts around myself, put the electrodes in their proper position, and pull the lever. By the lever I see the designation: WIRED FOR TWO-TWENTY. I say it again, "I AM CRUCIFIED WITH CHRIST!" (Gal. 2:20). I reckon it and it is so. But what of tomorrow when I am put-upon, weary, and short of patience? I am to be reminded again . . . "I am crucified," and the process is to be repeated.

It is here again that we will begin to praise the Lord anew for the cross. The cross is God's answer to the problem of self. On that cross Christ died. But something else happened there. We died with him! As we reckoned his death for us, our *sin* problem was cared for. As we reckon constantly our death with him, our *self* problem will be cared for. We can then reckon all of his life in us!

So there was a two-fold cross. An *outer* cross, the payment of sin's penalty, the death of the Substitute, to reconcile us to God was only one part of God's plan. When that cross becomes the *inner* cross applied to *self,* then there is new and complete liberty. "For he that is dead is freed from sin" (Rom. 6:7).

Let's allow L. E. Maxwell to provide a summary:

"From his original home and center in God, where God was his light and life, the very breath of his breath, the central sun of his universe . . . from this secret place of the Most High, man broke off and plunged out into the far country of self, into the alienation and night of separation from God. God has been cast down. Self has usurped the throne, a usurper who never abdicates. Self is the new and false center upon which man is fixed. He loves himself as nothing else under the sun. 'Self,' says William Law, 'is the root, the branches, the tree of all the evils of our fallen state.' When this nearly almighty self unseated and dethroned El Shaddai, what could God do? Herein is displayed the genius of God. The cross is indeed 'the power of God and the wisdom of God.' Calvary is God's ax laid at the root of the first family tree. Adam is cut off. A new Adam ascends the throne. The Lord Jesus came as the new head of a new race. He willingly came, came in the likeness of sinful flesh. With cords of selfless love, he fastened us to himself down to the very depths of death, all in order to clear away sin's penalty and persuade us to choose God instead of self. He chose to die, die for us, to die in our place, yea, to die our death . . . that he might save us from our sinful selves."[5]

Praise the Lord! Herein lies the cure to the problem of self. The enemy that blocked our path is now removed!

PART I
CHRISTIANITY IS CHRIST-IN-YOU-ITY

"Christ liveth in me; and the life which I now live in the flesh I live by the faith of the Son of God, who loved

THE KEY TO TRIUMPHANT LIVING

me, and gave himself for me" (Gal. 2:20).

There is a simple secret to the Christian life. It is, in fact, so simple that millions miss it. There is a dynamic so mighty that no life can remain the same after discovering it. Paul called it a "mystery which hath been hid from ages and from generations, but now is made manifest to his saints" (Col. 1:26). It is THE SECRET, THE KEY, THE SUPREME DYNAMIC, THE GLORIOUS SECRET of the Christian life. I bless the day I began to see it! True Christianity is simply "Christ-in-you-ity" and "Christ-in-me-ity."

DECISION

What happens when we make the decision to trust Christ as our personal Savior? This is a question we must answer if we are to understand how the Christian life operates. Becoming a Christian comes about by inviting Jesus Christ to come to live inside of us. Being a Christian simply means that the Christ who came to dwell in us is going about acting like himself in us. If I am a Christian, having invited Christ to live in my heart, I can say, "Jesus Christ is alive in my life right now!" I may not feel worthy of it. I may not understand it. I may not feel it all the time. But the blessed truth is that all the time, every night and day, at work and at play, when I feel down, and when I feel up . . . JESUS CHRIST IS ALIVE IN ME. When I decided to trust him as my Savior, he came to set up housekeeping in my life.

Once there lived another man within me,
    Child of earth and slave of Satan he;
But I nailed him to the cross of Jesus
    And that man is nothing now to me.

Now another Man is living in me,
   And I count his blessed Life as mine,
I have died to all my own life,
   I have risen to all his Life divine.

DILEMMA

Once a person becomes a Christian, he is faced with one monstrous dilemma. He is supposed to live, love, walk, and talk like Christ. He is commanded to love his enemies, abstain from the very appearance of evil, and grow in grace. Thus, we are to worry about nothing and be thankful for everything. We are ordered to rejoice always, deny ourselves, accept the fact of our death, and follow Christ every day of our lives. We are to set our affections on things above and not on things on the earth. Added to these and dozens of other demands made upon us, we are supposed to be of good comfort, cheerful, and kind in the midst of an unkind world. This is our dilemma. Paul reflected it when he said, "when I would do good, evil is present with me" (Rom. 7:21). He had already said, "I have a desire but how to perform I find not" (Rom. 7:18).

Finally Paul remonstrated, "It's hopeless!" What a discovery when we find that we *cannot* live the Christian life. A friend of mine said that he knew three stages of the Christian life. First, he went through the stage in which he thought the Christian life was *easy*. That didn't last long. The next stage through which he passed was one in which he felt the Christian life to be *difficult*. He found out soon that this was not true either. He then discovered that it was *impossible*. After discovering it to be impossible, he found it exciting! "O wretched man that I am! who shall deliver me from the body of this death?" was Paul's cry of despair with himself in Romans

7:24. He had discovered what every Christian must sooner or later discover who would know triumphant living. Have you given up on yourself? The whole human nature is geared against giving up. "Get in there and do your best!" is often our motto. Our best was not enough to get us saved, and our best will not be enough to get us to victory. In fact, our best, as much as we seem to revere it, is our enemy, in that: (1) It will never work and thus is a waste of time. (2) If it did work, we could take a part of the credit for our victory. (3) As long as we do our best, we disallow God from doing his normal in us! (This makes "our best" a terrible enemy.) We are not encouraged anywhere in the Bible to resort to our best. There is no evidence in the Scripture to be found that God expects anything of us but total and abject failure. This is the reason for the cross in our salvation and the cross in our inner life. Self would do its best and take the credit. Self can live a life that has some appearances of Christlikeness, but self cannot be Christlike. Our dilemma is clear . . . we cannot be what God desires and what the Bible requires. The great question is, "How to perform?"

DECLARATION

Christ is in you! *That* is the only hope of glory. The word "glory" has to do with value. It implies the coming to be what a thing was made to become. My hope of ever being what I was made to become is Christ living in me. This is the declaration which solves the dilemma. Christ *for* us is a gladdening fact. Christ *with* us is even more thrilling. But Christ *in* us is unspeakably glorious!

This is my wonderful story,
Christ to my heart has come.

Jesus, the King of glory
Finds in my heart a home.
Mystery hid from ancient ages,
But at length to faith made plain,
Christ in me the hope of glory,
Tell it o'er and o'er again.

Think of it . . . CHRIST IS IN US! He, who in the
earlier verses of Colossians 1, is . . .

The image of the Invisible God—(v. 15)
   The Creator—(v. 16)
      The Sustainer—(v. 17) is . . .
         The One in whom all fulness dwells—(v.
         19):

He Lives in me! Can you fathom it? Jesus said, "All
power is given unto me in heaven and in earth" (Matt.
28:18). This is the One who lives in you and me. This
is a truth beyond all our capacities to understand. It is
the prime fact of our faith. Our hope is in Christ indwelling our lives.

This moment finds man stationed on this little wayside
planet called Earth. The earth is swinging in an unchanging orbit around the sun at a speed of 66,000 miles per
hour. We are held to it by a power called gravity. The
centrifugal force exerted between the earth and the sun
has been approximated by the British Astronomical Soci-
ety to be the equivalent of 300 million tons. That is the
same as the breaking strain of a steel rod three thousand
miles in diameter. Yet, through the same air where those
mighty forces are exerted, a voice can be heard. A bird
can fly through it with the greatest of ease. What holds
it together?

The scientists cannot tell us. We know an answer the

scientists are still seeking. We know what holds the atoms together and keeps the world from burning up in a split second. We know what holds the universe and the galaxies in place. The answer is given in Colossians 1:17, "and by him all things consist." That is, by his power everything stands together in an ordered whole. If the power of my Savior were to be withdrawn from this universe for one second it would fly into chaos. AND THIS SAME JESUS LIVES INSIDE MY BODY TO BE MY LIFE. His life in me living, his love in me loving, and his mind in me thinking . . . this is my hope of glory!

This declaration is a plain fact of Scripture. Long before Paul wrote about it in his epistles, Jesus made clear the nature of our relationship with him. In speaking of the Spirit who was to be "another" Comforter, Jesus promised that "He . . . shall be in you" (John 14:17). When he used the word "another," he was speaking of one of the same kind as he, himself. There are two Greek words for "another." One means "another of a different kind" and the other (used in this case) "another of the identical kind." "I am sending you One just like Me" was the implication of Jesus.

Again Jesus said, "At that day ye shall know that I am in my Father, and ye in me, and I in you" (John 14:20). "That day" was a designation for the time when the Comforter would be sent. Further, Jesus said, "If a man love me, he will keep my words: and my Father will love him, and we will come unto him, and make our abode with him" (John 14:23). Jesus had already indicated his "secret" to the indwelling of the Father when he said, "the Father that dwelleth in me, he doeth the works" (John 14:10). If God was in the body of Christ doing the works, the consistency of the principle demands that God be in Christ *in me* doing the works. Now doesn't that take a load off? After years of working for God, fretting over details, struggling with feelings of inadequacy, and ending up very sick and very tired . . . isn't it good news that God is in you "both to will and to do of his good pleasure" (Phil. 2:13)?

How could we miss such an obvious fact of Scripture? Let us observe just a few of the Scriptures that tell us that we are indwelt:

Ephesians 3:16	That he would grant you, according to the riches of his glory, to be strengthened with might by his Spirit in the inner man.
Ephesians 3:17	That Christ may dwell in your hearts by faith.
Ephesians 3:20	Now unto him that is able to do exceeding abundantly above all that we ask or think, according to the *power* that worketh *in* us.
Colossians 1:29	Whereunto I also labour, striving according to his working, which worketh in me mightily.
Colossians 3:11	But Christ *is* all, and *in* all.
2 Corinthians 13:5	Examine yourselves, whether ye be in the faith; prove your own selves. Know ye not your own selves, how that Jesus Christ is *in* you, except ye be reprobates?
1 John 4:4	Ye are of God, little children, and have overcome them: because greater is he that is *in* you, than he that is in the world.
Ephesians 4:6	One God and Father of all, who is above all, and through all, and *in* you all.

Romans 8:9-11   But ye are not in the flesh, but in the Spirit, if so be that the Spirit of God dwell *in* you. Now if any man have not the Spirit of Christ, he is none of his. And if Christ be *in* you, the body is dead because of sin; but the Spirit is life because of righteousness. But if the Spirit of him that raised up Jesus from the dead dwell *in* you, he that raised up Christ from the dead shall also quicken your mortal bodies by his Spirit that dwelleth *in* you.

Christianity then is simply Jesus Christ living in our bodies minding his own business. When that concept dawns upon the Christian, it changes his whole life. It alters his outlook and disposition. It changes the nature of his work and worship.

DYNAMIC

It is this dynamic, Christ in you, which *secures our salvation.* If Christianity were nothing more than a man deciding to worship Jesus and doing his best to imitate him, there indeed would be little hope. But if Christianity is Jesus coming into an available human body and acting like himself, then there is abundant hope. In the one, all is based on human strength. In the other, all is based on the dynamic of the indwelling Christ. If my salvation depended on my ability to be like Christ, I could be lost again and again. But if my salvation depends on Jesus, then I cannot be lost. Thus my salvation is secured not by my imitation of Christ but by my *participation* in Christ. He, himself, living in me, is the security of my salvation. I need no other.

Not only is our salvation secured, but our *service is certified*. It bears the mark of divinity on it. I greatly fear that when the final accounting is done, much of the work that we have sought to do for God will not stand. It has been done in the flesh, with fleshly motives, and toward fleshly goals. Paul fearfully declares in Romans 14:23, "Whatsoever is not of faith is sin." Jesus said, "The Father that dwelleth in me, he doeth the works" (John 14:10). If Jesus depended on the Father *in* him to do the works, how much more should we depend upon him *in* us to do the works here? If Jesus freely admitted, "The Son can do nothing of himself," should we feel hesitant in making the same admission?

Man working for God is one thing. God working in man is quite another. What we have in our world is a system of religion that, in the main, encourages folks to work for God. This kind of work is bothersome, fruitless, and frustrating. I have known many people who were bored to death of church work. But when we face the glorious fact that "it is God who worketh in you," a new day dawns!

We are not in the world to bear witness to Christ through our own strength. Christ is in us in the world to bear witness of himself. The Christian life is not the doing of things to please God but the yielding of our bodies to God so that he can, through the indwelling Christ, do things for himself. No work, done in the flesh, bears the mark of divine certification. If Christ in us does the work, that work will stand when the stars have fallen.

The dynamic of this fact of Christ indwelling is found not only in *salvation secured, service certified,* but in *conquest complete.* In this great *key* (Christ in me), there is victory. Victory had eluded me until the hour I recognized this fact. My desire was such that if victory in the Christian life is a mountain peak toward which I struggle with all my human effort, then struggle I must; but if victory is a gift I receive in the Person of Jesus Christ, then my struggle is useless. "And this is the victory that overcometh the world, even our faith" (1 John 5:4). Victory is not *something* I win but *Someone* I receive into my life.

All that I have been but did not want to be is gone before him who walked into my life, who has no defilement in him. All that I have ever wanted to be and could not be, he comes to be in me. What I want to be to a world and cannot be, he comes to be in me: the Bread of Life, the Water of Life, the Light of the World, the Love of God. Tired of being busy *straining* and *complaining*, I find now that I can know joy in just *containing*. My hope of glory is just . . . CHRIST IN ME. Nobody can be like Jesus like Jesus can. He is in me. All of him is in me. All of him in me is available to me and through me to a lost world. That makes Christianity exciting. This makes it *Christ-in-you-ity* and *Christ-in-me-ity*.

DEMONSTRATIONS

All around us there are clear and living demonstrations of the vitality of indwelling. In the Scriptures and in our surroundings there are ample illustrations from which we can learn.

THE BODY AND ITS MEMBERS

Not only are our bodies the temples of God but we, all together, are the body of Christ. This is the church. "For we are members of his body, of his flesh, and of his bones" (Eph. 5:30). There is within the human body a vivid illustration of indwelling. I and my body are not two but one. My life is not an existence of two people dwelling, but one. My life is living in my body. We are one. All of my body, under normal circumstances, is subject to me. My thoughts, my energy, and my life indwell this body to every extreme part. Crush my little finger and I know about it. That is another part of me. Pinch my big toe and I am aware of it. That is another part of me. Pull a hair from my head and I feel it. All of these are parts of me because I indwell my body. This is not difficult to understand.

Christ dwells in his corporate body, the church. He also dwells in our individual bodies. It is his life in our individual bodies that makes the corporate body, the church, a living and vital spiritual organism. The entity that makes my body a unified body is myself indwelling it and controlling every member. In the same way Christ indwelling and controlling his corporate body makes it a glorious unity. Just as I can dwell in me, Christ can dwell in me individually. As he indwells me and controls me, I become an effectual member of the greater body, the church.

Look at your body. You live in it. It is your means of expression and transportation. Your hand is just another hand, but it is *your* hand available to you. When it goes to do a task, the simplest task is impossible without you. But you have found that when your hand makes itself available to you, all that you are becomes available to it. In reality it is you in that hand doing the work. The same with the feet and the legs, the eyes and the ears, and the whole body—there is restful availability on the part of the body to you.

Just as you live in your body, Christ, when invited, comes to live there too. As you reckon death to yourself and reckon his life in you, he becomes *Resident Lord*. The decisions you used to make, he now makes. The directions you were accustomed to choosing are now his choices. For you to live now is for Christ to live, because you have given your body to him as his means of expression and transportation. He goes where he likes, as he likes, when he likes. It is now his body. It is available to him. The marvelous mate truth to this is that he is available to your body. The miracle of mutual availability brings about abundance of life.

I find great joy each day with spiritual exercises. One of them goes something like this:

When I first look at myself in the morning, which is always quite a humbling experience, I remind myself, "This is not my body. It belongs to Jesus. It is available to him every moment of the day. I am dead. I reckon it so." I take my place in the chair of execution. I tighten the belts, put on the electrodes, activate the "220 Button" (Gal. 2:20) and "I AM CRUCIFIED WITH CHRIST." I then say to Jesus, "Lord, since I don't live anymore, you are free to live your life out in me. I claim my death and your life. Thank you that you are alive and well and resident in me. Thank you that no demand will be made on me today that is not made on you, that no problem will come that will not come to your wisdom's attention. On that basis, before this day really begins, I claim your life in me as my reason for being about to shout . . . 'Victory' . . . Now!"

A CORN OF WHEAT

"Verily, verily, I say unto you, Except a corn of wheat fall into the ground and die, it abideth alone: but if it die, it bringeth forth much fruit" (John 12:24). Here Jesus gives us another clear illustration of the vitality of indwelling.

The seed is just a seed. The glory of it is that it has life resident in it. It will never know its intended purpose until it is placed in those conditions conducive to death. You can take that seed, clean it, polish it, and mount it in a prominent place on the mantle. It would still be just a seed. There is life *in* but no life *through* it. It has not died. Try to preserve it and its glory is lost. Throw it unto the cold, damp ground and its glory will begin to come to pass.

So it is with the Christian. Here is just another life. The glory of the Christian life is that there is the Life of God in Christ resident in it by the Holy Spirit. Let that Christian "play it safe" and there is no glory. He can live cleanly, be moral and efficient, stand out for all to see, and even be "dedicated," but there is no glory. He is impressive but not miraculous; *but* he learns the secret! It is Christ *in* him that is the hope of glory! He takes death to himself and chooses to let the death-life principle become operative in his life. As he dies to himself, Christ begins to live through him. The agony he fears and the tragedy he faces give way to a victory he shares. The dying he thought would be an agony and a tragedy turns out to be a victory.

Christ was that corn of wheat. He did not attempt to make an exhibit of his life and save men thereby. It would take more than human life to save a sinful world. It required the life of God and that life, resident in Christ, could only be "poured out" as his body was broken. That seed "fell into the ground and died" and, indeed, it brought much fruit.

We are his seed in our world. His life is indwelling us. There is nothing amazing or miraculous about us in appearance. We are at our best when planted for his glory, because when we are planted, his life in us becomes his life sprouting through us and we bear much fruit in our world.

THE VINE AND THE BRANCH

"I am the vine, ye are the branches," Jesus reminded his disciples in John 15:5, and here he taught one of the clearest lessons about the indwelt life. The vine and the branch are one. There is one (the branch) dwelling in the other (the vine). All that the vine is, it is in the branch. Deal with the branch and you have dealt with the vine. All that the vine is and has is available to the branch.

The branch does not do the work of fruit-bearing but allows the vine to naturally bear fruit after its kind. If the branch could bear fruit of itself, it would not be after the kind of the vine. Its position is as Jesus reminds us, "For without me ye can do nothing" (John 15:5). The branch is useless to bear fruit without the vine. The vine is helpless to bear fruit without the branch. But the beautiful catalyst-truth is . . . *The Vine in the Branch is the hope of glory.* So the task of the branch is quite simple: it is to abide (remain restfully available) in the vine.

He is the Vine; we are the branches. We are expected to do nothing but abide, reckoning on a constant relationship to him in which all he is, is at work in us. Then we become more than impressive; we become miraculous! "If ye abide in me, and my words abide in you, YE SHALL ASK WHAT YE WILL, AND IT SHALL BE DONE UNTO YOU" (John 15:7). No wonder he went on to say, "These things have I spoken unto you, that *my* joy might remain in you, and that *your* joy might be full" (John 15:11).

The illustrations of the body and its members, the seed, and the vine and the branch came from the Scriptures. Three simple illustrations from life around us demonstrate the same truth.

THE AUTOMOBILE

There she sits. She is sleek and stylish, comfortable and powerful—the latest model automobile. She has horsepower to spare. What a sight as she gleams in the sun! A result of the best engineering know-how in the world, she is ready. But the glory of the automobile is not in its gleaming exterior or in the statistics about which the owner is prone to brag. As its name suggests, it was made for self-contained mobility. It has all the component parts . . . the alternator, the carburetor, the gears, pistons, radiator, wheels, and all the rest. But all these parts together are ineffectual in making the "auto-mobile." You can call it an "automobile" all day but it is not one until it "goes by itself."

Let's come to the catalyst-truth again. Intelligence in the automobile is not her hope of glory. She was made to be indwelt. Her component parts, her beauty, and her fuel are all alike . . . incapable of making her what she was made to become.

Here comes the driver. He enters and indwells; he takes over and retains control. His abiding in that automobile and that automobile abiding in him is her hope of glory. The beauty, the sleekness, the grace, and power take second place as the automobile moves out into the freeway "doing and being what she was designed to do and be." She is indwelt!

GOLFING PAR

I am not a golfer. I lived on a farm and ranch and had to walk miles after the cows. I never could see the future in knocking a little ball as far as you could and then having to go after it, only to repeat the same thing again. As far as I am concerned, the fellow had it right when he said that golf was:

The ineffectual endeavor . . . . .
   to put an insignificant ball . . . . .
      into an obscure hole . . . . .
         with completely inadequate instruments!

But it does make a good illustration. Let us suppose
that I had to play golf in order to go to heaven . . .
more than that, I had to shoot par. I am sure that I
could become much more adept than I am, but par would
put me in that class—"All have come short." I will promise you one thing, however. I would be found trying,
and trying hard. But I am sure that it would be the
same old story of hooking, slicing, topping, and marking
up the balls I didn't lose. But suppose one day someone
walked up to me while I was in a torrid practice session
and told me that there was a serum that could be injected
into the veins and, "ZAP," everything would be different.
Suppose I was told that the serum was the result of years
of research; that it contained the best of conditioning,
love for the game, driving, chipping, and putting from
all the great golfers of this century—Hogan, Player,
Snead, Palmer, Nicklaus, and all the rest. I am told further
that if I will give up on myself ever being a par golfer
and submit to this injection, by some miracle of metabolism my golfing becomes the consummate result of all
these great golfers as if they lived in me. They, dwelling
in me, would be my hope of par.

CHRIST DWELLING IN ME IS MY HOPE OF
GLORY. I fell below par on God's rating. I sinned and
came short of his glory. I could never make it on my
own. I could have tried for a hundred years but would
have been no closer at the end of that time than at the
beginning. Someone told me about a divine arrangement

whereby the living Lord Jesus would come to live on the inside of me and behave like himself in me. All that I had to do was give constant consent and obedience to the indwelling Christ. How beautiful is this arrangement! There is still in me that old "sub par" nature. But there lives in me another, Jesus Christ himself, and he is in control. That being so, my life becomes what it was made to be . . . an occasion for Jesus to live again in my world and love and serve that others might be brought to the Father.

TEA AND THE TEA BAG

Here is a cup of water and by it a tea bag. The water is not the tea and the tea is not the water. They are two separate items. The water is heated and the tea bag is placed in the water. A strange thing takes place . . . the water changes color and nature. It becomes indwelt by a new and dominant nature. The rich tea-color swirls around in the cup until the fluid is tea, not water. For the water to exist now is for tea to exist. The water could say, "It is no longer I that lives, but tea that lives in me." Not many people I know drink hot water. There isn't much of a demand for it. But if that water, heated in preparation, can be made to become a wholesome and stimulating drink, then it is worthwhile.

So the Christian is just a cup of water, which, when heated with faith and entered by the Savior, becomes something else. The Christ nature comes into him and with his consent dominates. He becomes more and more like Christ and less and less like himself. Just as the "tea in the water is the hope of taste," Christ in the Christian is the hope of glory!

And thus we have discovered the key to triumphant living . . . *CHRIST IN YOU THE HOPE OF GLORY!*

PART I
HOW WE FUNCTION

"And the very God of peace sanctify you wholly; and I pray God your whole SPIRIT and SOUL and BODY be preserved blameless unto the coming of our Lord Jesus Christ" (1 Thess. 5:23).

A funny thing happened to me on the way to this chapter! The telephone rang, and my secretary told me that a young lady had asked for an appointment. I was in the middle of Chapter 4. We set the appointment, and God quietly and dramatically confirmed through this young lady that this chapter should be written. The young lady's life was changed in a matter of moments when she began to realize what had happened to her. God used the information in this chapter to break through her depression and defeat and give us a testimony of victory.

You should know her better. We will not use her name because you might wish to put your name in at this point. She was saved and deeply involved in religious work, pouring her life out to other people. She ministered as a nurse in a little South Texas town. I knew her in the early days after her decision to follow God and spend her life among a minority group. At that time she was still enamored with the work which was the greatest challenge of her life. But, like so many people who serve the work of the Lord with great intentions, but find that the Lord of the work is not real, she soon began to tire. She became frustrated; fears, she never knew before, attacked her. She grew depressed, and she began to drive all the way to our city for frequent visits to the psychiatrist. This day she could go no further. She couldn't even drive home. She came into my study, the victim of utter despair with that "what-am-I-going-to-do?" look written all over her face.

It took only a few minutes for me to realize that the problem was a "religious work syndrome." There are thousands of people walking around with it. Some don't even know they have it. Well, she had the "walking" version of this illness. Before long it would have progressed into the "incapacitating" version. She had served the work of the Lord for a number of years. She had never known what it was to truly serve the Lord himself. She loved the work but had never learned to love the Lord as much as she loved the work. The work was more real to her than he was. Such serving, regardless of the quality of sincerity (and hers was real), results sooner or later in spiritual fatigue. When she found out how the Christian really functions, she bounded off her knees—after turning the work over to Jesus—with that "what-am-I-going-to-do?" look gone. Replacing it was an "I-can't-wait-to-see-what's-going-to-happen" countenance.

She is mentioned here because I fear that she represents thousands of people who have settled down to tolerate a malady believed to be incurable. Many of these people are in some form of church work who feel that "occupational hazards" force them to settle for a life less than abundant. I believe that as we understand how the human functions, we will be greatly aided in coming to victory in the Christian life.

If we are going to understand how we function, we must first know how we are designed. Every person is a *trinity* in that he has a body, a soul, and a spirit.

He has a *body* which puts him in contact with the outside world. He has a *soul* which contains a *spirit* with which he communicates with God and by which God speaks to him. The soul is at least threefold in its nature, involving the thought life (the *mind*), the volitional life (the *will*), and the emotions. God had told man that if he ate of the tree of knowledge of good and evil he would surely die. As long as he ate of the tree called Life, he would live. He made the fatal choice and, in a real sense, he died. Death reigned. Down in his spirit where God communed with him and spiritual life was real . . . he died. He no longer lived "in the spirit." We call what happened "the Fall" because man literally fell to a lower form of life than he had known with God in the garden. He must now live in his "soul," depending upon himself, his own judgment, and his own efforts. He is lost! He needs to be saved! Jesus came to seek and save that which was lost. He proposes to do that by coming to live in us! As he comes to live in us, something very vital happens

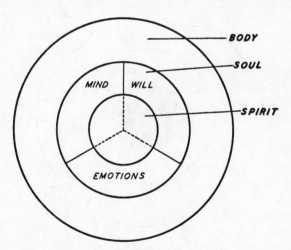

THE MAKEUP OF MAN [6]

to how we function. It will help for us to rehearse here the whole process of salvation.

WHAT IS THE CONDITION OF THE LOST MAN? (The Natural Man)

1. He is dead at the center of his being.
2. He is "put upon" by circumstances in his world.
3. He is shaped by his environment.
4. He is indwelt of the "unholy spirit" (Satan).

Man is alive in his mind, so he senses need. He is alive in his emotions, thus desires and longs for some better life. His volition is alive, so he may decide for Christ. Christ can be invited to live in the spirit that was made originally to contain the life of God. When this happens, the natural (lost) man is saved.

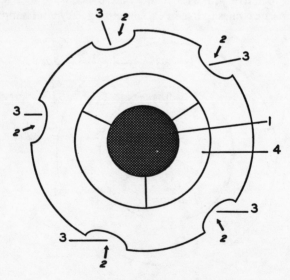

THE NATURAL MAN[7]

Now, we have already discovered that there are two kinds of saved people: the carnal (under the control of self), and the spiritual (under the control of Christ). Let's see the difference in these two in the following diagrams:

THE CARNAL MAN

1. He has come alive inside and Jesus has come to dwell.

2. He is weak and still subject to outside influences.

3. He still may be shaped by his world and the peer group.

4. He is attacked by Satan and has little defense.

5. He has trouble with priorities.

6. He is a fragmented person, trying to make the best of both worlds. He has much trouble with decisions. This is how he makes decisions: he calls all his fragmented selves to a committee meeting. He has a religious self, a social self, an economic self, a family self, and others. The main business comes up for consideration. He seeks to "chair the board" but no one seems to agree. Whatever is under consideration, his various "selves" pull in the direction of their own interests. What seems to be the best religiously is a poor move financially. That which seems to be acceptable socially does not agree with family self. A decision is reached but it is never unanimous. He has sought to have a *democracy* in his inner life. What he needs is a *Christocracy* (total Christ rule).

Now, let's not be mistaken about this *carnal* Christian. He or she may not be a backslider in the estimation of his friends. He or she may be a church worker. The *carnal* Christian is *any person who is not submitted to the total rule of Christ in his life.* We have talked about this person before in a previous chapter and have discovered him

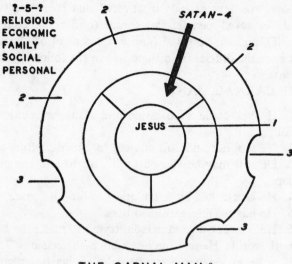

?-5-?
RELIGIOUS
ECONOMIC
FAMILY
SOCIAL
PERSONAL

SATAN-4

JESUS

THE CARNAL MAN [8]

or her to be anyone who has settled for less than all of Christ in all of the life.

THE SPIRITUAL MAN

1. He has effected a total "sellout" to Christ.

2. He has died to himself.

3. He has taken up the fact of his death and lives with it daily.

4. He experiences the same onslaughts of Satan and the world (and worse) but is not overcome.

5. He has an inner strength which seems to penetrate through his entire personality and pervade every area of his life.

6. He has enthroned Christ in his life and now Christ presides over his entire personality.

The *residing* Christ becomes the *presiding* Christ.

The *resident* Christ becomes the *reigning* Christ!

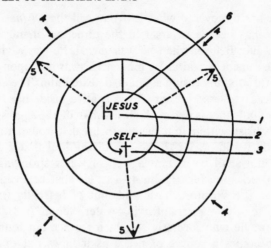

THE SPIRITUAL MAN [9]

THE DIVINE FLOW IN THE SPIRITUAL MAN

This fellow has found the secret:

1. At the center of his being he has come alive in Christ.

2. That Christ who has come to live in the center of his being is acknowledged as the Lord.

3. From His position as Lord he exerts his supremacy over the soul. The mind comes to be indwelt with the mind of Christ.

4. The will comes to be taken over by the will of Christ.

5. The emotions are pervaded by the authority of Christ.

6. The soul becomes the "blessed captive" of the risen Christ.

7. The body becomes the occasion of Christ expressing himself. A change in metabolism takes place. There is more bounce in the step, more joy on the face, and more delight in the life.

He has discovered what I love to call the *Divine Flow*. There has been a reversal in the direction of influence in his life. Before, when he was carnal, he was a victim of the outside world as its influences swarmed upon him and, through unceasing assaults, defeated him. The *secret* he has discovered is that Christ is alive inside him. The flow of influence is reversed. He is a man on the aggressive. The Christ within him begins to break through to the outside world. ". . . the water [divine life] that I shall give him shall be in him a well of water springing up into everlasting life" (John 4:14). "He that believeth on me, as the scripture hath said, out of his belly (inner man) shall flow rivers of living water" (John 7:38).

Now, he who formerly sought for peace but found it not becomes a source of peace as it flows out of him like a river. He who sought for love and was starved for it becomes a river of love! He who longed for the fruit of the Spirit becomes himself a number of rivers. The promise of Jesus was that he would become . . . not a little stream, or a little brook, and not even just *a* river but RIVERS OF LIVING WATER.

How do we function? We were made to contain the life of God. Man was disqualified and, therefore, lost that inner quality of life in the garden. Christ came to restore all that man had lost. When invited to live in the human spirit, he comes as *the* Spirit of God to live. As he is allowed to be the reigning Lord, he exercises his blessed Lordship not only in the deep of man's spirit but in the soul, the domain of the mind, the will, and the emotions. The whole body in reality then belongs to Jesus for his use and glory. For the first time, we begin to see how God made the human to function. Man can be impressive without Jesus as Lord, but man cannot be miraculous without Jesus as Lord. And in the final

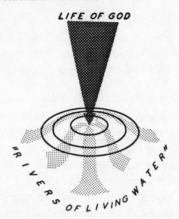

THE DIVINE FLOW IN THE SPIRITUAL MAN [10]

accounting we are worth no more than what our lives show the world about God. Do you desire to function as you are made to function? Then turn it over to Jesus!

PART 1
THE TWOFOLD LIFE

"For if, when we were enemies, we were reconciled to God by the death of his Son, MUCH MORE, being reconciled, we shall be saved by his life" (Rom. 5:10).

In spiritual things it is especially true that we learn by repetition. Thus we discover that as we are confronted by the verities of the Christian life, we will find the same truths repeated in different terms. I have found special significance in observing the Christian life as a TWO-FOLD LIFE. For years I could see only one facet. When I saw or heard the term "Jesus Saves," I could only think of missing hell or making heaven. This is only a part of what being saved means. Thus a lot of folks are not experiencing much heaven on the way to heaven. Let us observe some of the illustrations of the twofold life.

LIFE AND LIFE MORE ABUNDANTLY

Jesus said, "I am come that they might have life, and that they might have it more abundantly" (John 10:10). At first glance, one might pass over the twofoldness of this glorious statement. There are definitely two facets of our salvation to be seen here. In the one, we have life. But, alas, some have life and no more. They are uncomfortable and carnal. They are heaven bound but not heaven happy here and now. Jesus came that we might not only *have* life, but the *manner* in which we have it is significant. Many people have life who do not have it more abundantly. Many people have life; some people have it more abundantly. There is a vast difference. Which do you have?

RECONCILIATION AND SAVING LIFE

"For if, when we were enemies, we were *reconciled* to God by the death of his Son, MUCH MORE, being reconciled, we shall be saved by his life" (Rom. 5:10). In the work of redemption there are two glorious works . . . the death of Christ and the resurrection of Christ. Neither can be ignored in the life of victory. Because of the death of Christ, we have received the atonement. Thus we are reconciled to God, but we need more than mere reconciliation. We need a new life, a new dynamic. What Jesus provides for us in his death is one facet of salvation. What he provides for us in his life is another! If all we had was reconciliation with God, it would be glorious. But we have more . . . much more.

We have *Christ himself,* living in us.

We are saved from sin because he died for us.

   We can be saved from self because he is living in us.

We have reconciliation and are on our way to heaven because he died for us. We have VICTORY and thus have heaven in our hearts because of the presence of Jesus' saving life.

IN CHRIST AND CHRIST IN US

"And be found in him, not having mine own righteousness, which is of the law, but that which is through the faith of Christ, the righteousness which is of God by faith" (Phil. 3:9). In this verse we see our position *in Christ.* We have been placed into Christ by the Holy Spirit; "For by one Spirit are we all baptized into one body" (1 Cor. 12:13). In one glorious act, the Holy Spirit immersed us into Christ. Paul further confirms this in Romans 6:3, "Know ye not, that so many of us as were baptized into Jesus Christ were baptized into his death?" Jesus further clarifies our position when he says, "Abide in me, and I in you" (John 15:4). There is no doubt that we are IN CHRIST.

But this is only half the story of our glorious life as Christians. He is in us. ". . . Christ liveth in me . . ." (Gal. 2:20); ". . . Christ in you, the hope of glory" (Col. 1:27). Many a Christian rejoices in only a half-salvation. He knows he is in Christ but has never awakened to the fact that Christ is in him. Let's look at the two facets together:

   We are in him for forgiveness.
      He is in us for vitality of life.
   We are in him for protection.

He is in us for power.

We are in him for heaven later on.

He is in us to bring heaven here and now.

We are in him for salvation.

He is in us for satisfaction.

REST AND SOUL REST

It took me more than twenty years to see the *twofoldness* of the beautiful passage in Matthew 11:28-30. "Come unto me, all ye that labour and are heavy laden, and I will give you rest" (v. 28). There is immediate rest to that one who responds to the Savior's invitation. What a sweet rest it is! That would be enough to justify our coming to him. That is the rest of becoming, the rest of forgiveness, the rest of union, experience, relationship. But there is more. "Take my yoke upon you, and learn of me: for I am meek and lowly in heart: and ye shall find REST UNTO YOUR SOULS" (v. 29). The old-time preachers were accustomed to speaking of SOUL REST. The world is tired and seeking rest today. The rest of forgiveness and the rest of the soul are two differing qualities. The one depends on coming to Jesus . . . the other depends on taking the yoke of Jesus. Many have come to Jesus for the rest of forgiveness who have not taken the yoke of Jesus. The yoke is a symbol of submission. Some who know Jesus as Savior are not living lives of submission to him and thus do not have soul rest. Only within the context of the yoke of Christ can we really learn of him. When I was a boy my father had two great black work horses. There was much work to be done. These horses belonged to my father, but there was no way for them to know the mind of my father. He could have given them study courses with the finest of visual aids, but they could never have "learned of him." But, in a little room in the barn there was a set of harnesses. I watched my father as he went to the harness room, and I watched the horses as they submitted to the harnessing procedures. It looked complicated to my little mind. Then, when it was all done, dad would hook the horses to the plow and those two horses learned more about my father's will, mind, and desires in five minutes than they could have in five years outside the harness.

Christian, you can study the Gospels and the Epistles and add to that all the stories of the life of a Christian ever written, but one hour within the yoke of Christ will teach you more than all of this. Submission is the secret to learning and rest.

We saw earlier that Canaan is the spiritual symbol of the Christ-controlled life. It is the land of rest. The rest is not "from" labor but "in" labor. Discovering "rest unto the soul" is the unspeakable joy which comes to the life when Christ takes over. The Israelites had rest from the oppression of the Egyptian taskmasters, but they did not have the rest of Canaan. In Hebrews 3:18-19 we read, "And to whom sware he that they should not enter into his *rest*, but to them that believed not? So we see that they could not enter in because of unbelief." They missed the final rest because of unbelief and disobedience.

A later verse says, "There remaineth therefore a rest to the people of God. For he that is entered into his rest, he also hath ceased from his own works, as God did from his" (Heb. 4:9-10). This blessed soul rest has often been called *second rest*. The only way to find this rest "unto the soul" is to take his yoke. This simply means that we must accept the authority of his Lordship and acknowledge him as the boss of our lives. My only business in the Christian life is to make my life available to the boss of the business. The whole business of my life is his business. But how often do we want to worry about his business? Hence, there is no rest. But when I make it my business to make all my life his business, then I have no business worrying about the business. (You might need to read that again!) For an interesting experience, ask the next person you see who is a Christian this question, "Brother (or sister), do you have the REST?" The answer you will get may be interesting indeed. If he or she has the REST, what fellowship you both can have. If not, what a witness you can have.

Brother, do *you* have the REST?

RECEIVING AND WALKING

"As ye have therefore *received* Christ Jesus the Lord, so *walk* ye in him" (Col. 2:6). Here is another beautiful example of *twofoldness*. The mate verse of this is in 1 John 2:6, "He that saith he abideth in him ought himself also so to walk, even as he walked." Many Christians who have *received* are not *walking*. Notice that the first word of the first reference is "as," which is another way of saying, "in the same manner." How did we receive him? We gave up to him and asked him into our lives. We did not try, we trusted. As we trusted him to come in, we trust him in the experience of walking. We are not to walk "for" him as much as we are to walk "in" him. That is, just as we were saved by abandoning ourselves to him, we are overjoyed as we have the blessed relationship of walking "in" him. The carnal Christian has received Christ but is not walking in him. The spiritual Christian has both received and is walking in him.

PEACE WITH GOD AND THE PEACE OF GOD

The Bible is loaded with illustrations of the twofold life. Here is one of the most meaningful ones in the Bible. One facet is presented in Romans 5:1. "Therefore being justified by faith, we have peace *with* God through our Lord Jesus Christ." To have peace with God is marvelous, but this is not all we have when we have Jesus. Peace that is vital is more than a truce. It must be a relationship throbbing with life and purpose. There is more than peace *with* God.

There is the peace *of* God, as evidenced in Colossians 3:15, "And let the *peace of God* rule in your hearts, to the which also ye are called in one body; and be ye thankful." And again we see it in Philippians 4:7, "And the *peace of God,* which passeth all understanding, shall keep your hearts and minds through Christ Jesus." To have peace WITH God is one thing . . . to have the peace *OF* God as the garrison of our minds and hearts is surpassingly something else.

RIGHTEOUSNESS AND HOLINESS

How many times do we mistakenly make these two words synonymous! They are both vital, but they are not the same. Righteousness comes before holiness in the order of redemption. One (righteousness) is imparted to us through the death of Jesus on the basis of our act of faith. The other (holiness) is imputed to us through the life of Christ in the indwelling Spirit on the basis of the continuing work of the Spirit. What Jesus does in his death to make us righteous, he does in his life indwelling us to make us holy. We are declared righteous when we are saved. We cannot be holy until we are surrendered wholly to Jesus Christ. We cannot be holy by trying. We can be holy only by being filled with the *Holy Spirit.* The sufficiency of Christ is further presented as Paul says in 1 Corinthians 1:30, "But of him are ye in Christ Jesus, who of God is made unto us wisdom, and RIGHTEOUS-NESS and SANCTIFICATION [Holiness], and redemption."

SAVING FAITH AND SATISFYING FAITH

Many people who are saved are not satisfied. The experience of salvation is not just an event; it is a relationship. Just as faith was needed in the initial event, it is needed in the continuing relationship. Paul, in Romans 5:1, speaks of a saving faith by which "we have peace with God." But in the next verse he adds an "also." As we are saved by an initial act of faith we continue in faith to have "access by faith into this grace wherein we stand . . ." (Romans 5:2a).

It is in the "much more" that we find the victory in Christ. Faith is the trusting commitment of self to Jesus Christ. It is the disposition of faith that brings us to salvation as an experience in life. It is continued faith that brings us to complete satisfaction in an unceasing relationship with our Lord. How right and relevant John was when he said, "and this is the victory that overcometh the world, even our faith" (1 John 5:4).

UNION AND POSITION

In the matter of salvation there is *union* truth and there is *position* truth. Union truth has to do with what happened at the time of conversion. Position truth has to do with what happens afterward. We are generally long on union truth and woefully short on position truth. There are many scriptures that could be used here, but there is none better than the John 15 discourse on the vine and the branches. It is dangerous to emphasize union truth without going on to enlarge on position truth. The result of such an emphasis is seen everywhere today in the church. Most Christians, when asked to share their experience with Christ, will tell what happened years ago and have little to say about what happened last week. They live in view of the union, but the present position means very little.

Both of these areas of truth are treasure-filled, but union truth without position truth is *joyless* and position truth without union truth is *baseless.* Together they complement each other. In union, the branch is grafted into the vine. In position, the life of the vine flows through the branch. The relationship does not *end* with the engrafting; it merely *begins.* Thus, what we see here is simply another way of saying what we have said before about the twofold life.

In union we have *life . . .* in position we have *life more abundantly.* In union we are *reconciled . . .* in position we have his *saving life.* In union we are *in Christ . . .* in position we enjoy *Christ in us.* In union we have *rest . . .* in position we have *soul rest.* In union we *receive* Christ *. . .* in position we are *walking with Christ.* In union we have peace *with* God *. . .* in position we have the peace *of* God. In union we have *righteousness . . .* in position we have *holiness.* In union we have the result of *saving* faith *. . .* in position we have the results of *satisfying* faith.

Many people have the certainty of *union* with Christ who do not enjoy the joys of *position.* Instead of living in the victory of position they live in their *conditions.* These vary with circumstances and are greatly affected by feelings. To live in circumstances is to live defeated. To live in our position is to live in victory because our position is perfect. "Blessed be the God . . . who hath blessed us with all spiritual blessings in heavenly places in Christ" (Eph. 1:3).

HIS DEATH FOR US AND OUR DEATH IN HIM

Another expression of the twofold life is observed in what happened at Calvary. Christ died for us as our representative. If he was our substitute, then we, representatively, died with him. The doctrine of co-crucifixion is absolutely vital to the life of victory. While his death *for* us secures our *relationship,* our death *with* him procures our *fellowship.* (And therein is another twofold expression.) As we reckon our death with him, this makes way for his resurrected life to indwell us and control us. For this reason Paul exhorts us, "Reckon ye also yourselves to be dead indeed unto sin, but alive unto God through Jesus Christ our Lord" (Rom. 6:11).

Dr. A. B. Simpson says, "The death of Christ simply means that when He died, I died, and in God's view I am now as if I had been executed for my own sins, and am now recognized as another person who has risen with Christ, and has been justified from his former sins because he has been executed for them. Beloved, have you entered into the death of Christ and counted it yours, and through it, are you now alive unto Him in the power of His resurrection?"

> Buried with Christ and raised with him, too,
> What is there left for me to do?
> Simply to cease from struggling and strife,
> Simply to walk in newness of life.
> Living with Christ, who dieth no more,
> Following Christ, who goeth before.
> I am from bondage utterly freed,
> Reckoning self, as dead indeed.[11]

BORN OF THE SPIRIT AND FILLED WITH THE SPIRIT

Jesus talked with Nicodemus in John 3 about being born of the Spirit. This is that mighty act of the Spirit of God by which we are brought into the family of God. Again, we must emphasize that this is only the beginning of our relationship in God's great family. Since we have become the children of God by the new birth, how shall we live like children of God? The answer is found in the continued working of the Holy Spirit in our lives. We are to be "filled with the Spirit" (Eph. 5:18). This means that we are to be controlled, guided, and motivated by the same Holy Spirit which made our spiritual birth a reality. We shall deal with this more fully later on.

BECOMING AND BEING

In summary we must joyfully conclude that the Christian life is both balanced and thorough. It includes decision as well as direction. It is an event followed by a process. But thousands upon thousands of Christians have never discovered the "much more" that the Bible speaks of. We speak much of becoming a Christian but very little about how to be what we have become.

On the one side we *become* Christians through:

>   . . . the death of Christ;
>   . . . justification by faith;
>   . . . conversion;
>   . . . taking a step;
>   . . . being born of the Spirit.

On the other, we are able *to be what we have become* through:

>   . . . the indwelling life of Christ;
>   . . . sanctification by the Spirit;
>   . . . appropriation;
>   . . . continuing a walk;
>   . . . being filled with the Spirit.

Paul's epistles generally deal with how to be what we have become. In Romans is a clear presentation of a balanced preaching aimed at getting people to become Chris-

tians as well as teaching them how to be what they had
become.

The teaching and preaching today that ignores *being*
and emphasizes *becoming* may bring about conversion
but cannot produce discipleship.

This volume deals with how to be what we have
become.

There are more illustrations of the twofoldness of our
life with Christ. The reader will find it a rewarding study
to look for more. We have observed these examples that
we might more fully appreciate the completeness of our
salvation. It is toward the "full salvation" or "balanced
life" that we are studying.

PART II
THE REIGN OF CHRIST OVER THE HUMAN LIFE

"That he might be Lord both of the dead and living"
Romans 14:9

"CHRIST IS ALL, AND IN ALL."
Colossians 3:11

"O Christ, we crown thee Lord of all, in all our hearts
today;
We yield to thee our love, our life, our thoughts, our
will, our way.
Lord, take and use us as thou wilt; make every heart
thy throne,
And let our every ransomed power be thine and thine
alone."

A. B. SIMPSON

JESUS IS LORD

"And that every tongue should confess that Jesus Christ is Lord, to the glory of God the Father" (Phil. 2:11).

If discovering Christ to be *resident* in the believer can be likened to finding the key to triumphant living, then discovering the *reign* of Christ can be likened to the key opening the lock of life. The lordship of Christ is the pivot around which the whole matter of triumph in the Christian life revolves. Until his lordship becomes a constant reality in the life, there can be no fullness. Many have known and enjoyed the riches of the discovery of Christ as personal Savior. And while it is true that Christ cannot be accepted by degrees, many have never known the completeness of joy in living under his lordship. To have him as Savior is wonderful. To know him as Savior *and Lord* is infinitely more wonderful!

The lordship of Christ is the grand design of redemption. Paul proclaims this in Romans 14:9, "For to this end Christ both died, and rose, and revived, THAT HE MIGHT BE LORD BOTH OF THE DEAD AND LIVING."

The lordship of Christ is the master motivation and the royal resource from which the Christian is to witness. "All power (authority) is given to me in heaven and in earth. . . . Go ye therefore . . ." (Matt. 28:18-19).

The lordship of Christ is the apex toward which all lines of history are moving to finally converge. "That in the dispensation of the fulness of times he might gather together in one all things in Christ, both which are in heaven, and which are on earth; even in him" (Eph. 1:10).

The lordship of Christ is the prime purpose of God for the program of the church and Christian living. "And he is the head of the body, the church: who is the beginning, the firstborn from the dead; THAT IN ALL THINGS HE MIGHT HAVE THE PREEMINENCE [Lordship]" (Col. 1:18).

The lordship of Christ is the catalyst of this volume, joining the vital *residence of Christ in the life* to the culminating *release of Christ through the life*.

The lordship of Christ (glorification) is the great secret in connecting the glory of the risen and ascended Lord to the pouring out of the Holy Spirit. This is a secret of such significance that Jesus mentions it in the prospect of his dying and coming glorification, and Peter mentions it in retrospect to explain the sequence of divine history. Jesus said in John 7:39, ". . . for the Holy Ghost was not yet ['given' is not in the original]; because that Jesus was not yet glorified." Then Peter states in Acts 2:33,36: "Therefore being by the right hand of God exalted, and having received of the Father the promise of the Holy Ghost, he hath shed forth this, which ye now see and hear. Therefore let all the house of Israel know assuredly, that God hath made that same Jesus, whom ye have crucified, both Lord and Christ." We shall come to this later as it relates to the personal experience with the Holy Spirit.

The lordship of Christ is a personal discovery of such magnitude that no part of the life of the discoverer can ever be the same.

To live in the continuing light of the lordship of Christ is to know unceasing adventure. The disciples were always finding new expressions of his lordship. They found him to be Lord over simple problems as well as complex. They watched him turn water into wine, and the Scripture relates that he ". . . manifested forth his glory; and his disciples believed on him" (John 2:11). Every time he manifested his lordship, it must have been like coming to know him all over again. They forgot quickly, but he continued to forge a chain of evidence, link by link, around his lordship. He proved himself Lord over the elements as he arose to rebuke the wind. He demonstrated his lordship over death as he called the dead back to life. He asserted his lordship over disease as he healed all sorts of human maladies. He had already proved himself "mighty in battle" as he met the highest motivations Satan had to offer in the "lust of the flesh, the lust of the eyes, and the pride of life," and soundly defeated the subtle saboteur.

He exhibited his lordship over human scorn and hate and submitted to the cross with a love that only God could know as he said, "Father, forgive them, for they know not what they do" (Luke 23:34). His disciples believed on him with deepened faith at each encounter in which he proved his preeminence.

Then came the greatest test of all. He gave up his life on the cross. Body and spirit were separated. The last enemy held its prey for three days. Then, early in the morning, the spirit of my Savior entered that still body, and he became the "first-fruit of them that slept." He neatly wrapped the graveclothes and laid them aside. He then broke Caesar's seal and walked out of the tomb with the keys to death and hell swinging at his girdle. HE IS LORD OVER DEATH!

> Death could not keep its prey,
>   Jesus, my Saviour;
> He tore the bars away,
>   Jesus, my LORD!

Jesus is Lord! He is Lord of time and eternity. He was before all creation and will be around to announce the end of time. He is alpha and omega, the beginning and the end.

He is Lord of life, death, and judgment. He said, "I am the way, the truth, and the life" (John 14:6); ". . . I am the resurrection, and the life . . ." (John 11:25); "I . . . have the keys of hell and of death" (Rev. 1:18). Because of this, there is no judgment to those who are in him.

He is the Lord of history past and history future. Angels have announced him as Lord, and men have crowned him as Lord. God has declared him to be Lord.

If the minds of people everywhere could grasp this colossal fact in only a fraction of its glory, there would be shouting in the streets, in statehouses, and in hovels. Jesus is Lord! It changes the meaning of the past, the present, and the future. It changes the meaning of current events, dissolves the reasons for our greatest concerns, and causes hope to burn brightly in every heart.

He is Lord! Let the nation believe it and it will find a new soul. Let the church find it and there will be kindled a new fire. Let the individual discover it and he will have a new life.

This lordship is not untried. It has been challenged often and defeated never. It is not delicate and tottering; it has withstood the worst hell has to offer and stands firmer than ever before. The throne, often attacked, has never toppled. It still stands in awesome power.

The preacher in Ecclesiastes declared in the frivolous days of his youthful life . . .

"*Learning* is Lord," only later to say, "In much study is much weariness of the flesh."

"*Laughter* is Lord,"—later to say, "It is mad."
"*Liquor* is Lord," but to find no peace.
"*Luxury* is Lord," to discover all to be vanity.
"*Lust* is Lord," but there was no satisfaction.

Finally, a disillusioned old man, then wiser, said, "Let us hear the conclusion of the whole matter: Fear God, and keep his commandments: for this is the whole duty of man" (Eccl. 12:13). I tell you, "JESUS IS LORD."

> Jesus shall reign where e'er the sun
>   Does his successive journeys run;
> His kingdom spread from shore to shore,
>   Till moons shall wax and wane no more.

Charles Lamb was right when he said, "If all of the illustrious men were together and Shakespeare should enter their shining company, they would all rise to do him honor. But if Jesus should come, they would kneel and worship him."

Napoleon was right when he confessed, "I tell you, I know men, and jesus is not a man. Comparison is impossible between him and any other being in the world. He is truly a being by himself."

When Emerson was asked why he did not include Jesus among his list of representative men, he replied that the glistening garments of glory that Jesus wore caused him to believe that it took too much strength of constitution to compare him with other men. He cannot be compared with other men. HE IS LORD!

Why do we believe that he is Lord?

GOD GAVE HIM THE NAME

Men and angels have various names for Christ. Isaiah says, "His name shall be called Wonderful, Counsellor,

The mighty God, The everlasting Father, The Prince of Peace" (Isa. 9:6). John the Baptist pointed to him and said, "Behold the Lamb of God, which taketh away the sin of the world" (John 1:29). Matthew said, "And Jacob begat Joseph the husband of Mary, of whom was born Jesus, who is called Christ" (Matt. 1:16). The angel came to Joseph and announced, "Fear not to take unto thee Mary thy wife: for that which is conceived in her is of the Holy Ghost. And she shall bring forth a son, and thou shalt call his name JESUS: for he shall save his people from their sins" (Matt. 1:20-21). And she brought forth her firstborn son and called his name Jesus.

But when the God of heaven gave him a name . . . it was LORD! He is *Christ* because he is the Messiah, promised of old. He is *Jesus* because he is the Savior and Son of God. HE IS LORD . . . BECAUSE GOD HAS EXALTED HIM AND GIVEN HIM THAT NAME. It is a flat and decisive statement of Scripture that, "Wherefore God also hath highly exalted him, and given him a name which is above every name" (Phil. 2:9). God has made Him LORD.

ALL WILL ONE DAY CALL HIM LORD

It is a fact of future history that every knee will bow and every tongue will boldly declare that he is Lord. This is not a guess, not a venture, but a fact of prophecy which makes it as certain as if it had already happened.

It will be seen and heard in heaven. Dear old Noah, Moses, Abraham, Isaiah, Ezekiel, Daniel and all the rest will join in the chorus. Jesus is Lord!

It will be seen and heard in earth. When it happens, all the rulers of the earth, all the men of means around the world, all the potentates and princes will call him Lord.

It will be seen and heard in hell. Satan will bow his head and finally admit it, "Jesus is Lord!" Tom Paine will join in the chorus with Hitler and Voltaire and hell's sad choir will shout, "Jesus Christ is Lord!"

Say it in times of joy, "Jesus Christ is Lord!" Lest we be sidetracked with lesser joys, preoccupied with lesser gladness, caught up more with the blessing than the Blesser, acknowledge him as Lord.

Say it in times of sadness, "Jesus is Lord!" These times are but for a moment. Joy comes in the morning. Trouble is temporary. He is Lord forever. Let it ring in times of distress, "Jesus is Lord!"

Say it in times of bereavement, "Jesus is Lord!" When death's shadow has stolen over our homes, is there any more glorious a fact? A loved one is gone—a chair is vacant. A heart is longing and crushed, but Jesus is Lord!

Say it in times of pressure, "Jesus is Lord!" Who is He? He is the Lord! Where is He? Indwelling his own! Is there any pressure outside that is greater than he is inside? NO! "Greater is he that is in you" (1 John 4:4).

Say it in times of success, "Jesus is Lord!" As human applause deafens you, as men would lift you up to heaven and crown you Lord, refuse it and hand the crown to him. Beware, the Lord our God is one God. His glory he will not give to another. Jesus is Lord!

Say it in times of decision, "Jesus is Lord!" This is not your decision because your life is not yours. It is his alone! He is the way; walk in him. He is the truth; believe him. He is the life; let him live that life in your body. His decision is already made. You owe him your blind and complete obedience. He is Lord of that decision.

Say it in times of loneliness, "Jesus is Lord!" Is the family gone and have friends forsaken you? You may be lonely but you are not alone. "My Lord is near me all the time." "He will never leave me or forsake me." "If he is for us, who can be against us?"

Say it in times of confusion, "Jesus is Lord!" You have lost your way. You no longer have any idea what is important and what is not. You don't understand any more. You cannot feel anything. You are bothered, baffled, and bewildered. Shout it, "Jesus is Lord!"

Say it in times of crushing guilt, "Jesus is Lord!" Is your head bowed down low in sorrow and despair? You are self-discovered, self-dejected, and self-disgusted. You have fallen and failed again. Hear the words and say them again, "Jesus is Lord!"

Say it in times of accusation, "Jesus is Lord!" He is the Lord, Wonderful Counsellor. He understands. That is all that matters. Let the devil rage and roar like a lion. Let him accuse and deceive the world. But the Savior is King of Glory who tramples the young lion under his feet. He is the same . . . yesterday, today, and forever.

Say it in times of overwhelming challenge, "Jesus is Lord!" Is the task too great? Is the sum too high? Is the strength demanded too much? Is there no logical way it can be done? Is the risk too risky, the challenge too challenging? If it were not that the Lord was on our side, we would have fought in vain. "Be ye steadfast, unmoveable, always abounding in the work of the Lord, forasmuch as ye know that your labour is not in vain in the Lord" (1 Cor. 15:58).

Say it in times of family trouble, "Jesus is Lord!" Disharmony reigns. Misunderstanding prevails. Tempers flare. Communication is lost. Stalemates deadlock. Gloom settles. Positions are taken and battle lines are drawn. Hope fades. Panic threatens. Listen! Jesus is Lord! "Where the Spirit of the Lord is, there is *liberty*" (2 Cor. 3:17).

Say it when death threatens, "Jesus is Lord!" The doctor says that your time is measured. The heart misses, the blood slows, the chest rattles, the body cools, and death comes near. You need not go *under* death. You may go *over* it. For you are more than conqueror through him that loved you, and nothing shall separate you from the love of Christ. Do you remember the promise, "And whosoever liveth and believeth in me shall never die" (John 11:26)? Can you say with Paul, "O death, where is thy sting? O grave, where is thy victory? But thanks be to God, which giveth us the victory through our Lord Jesus Christ" (1 Cor. 15:55,57)? Jesus is Lord!

Say it when the last trumpet sounds, "Jesus is Lord!" The graves are opening. There is a shout from heaven and a trumpet blast. The archangel's voice is heard. This must be the day! Jesus is Lord!

His lordship is reasonable, real, and reliable. Accept this lordship and God's plan will be perfected in your life; God's purposes will be carried out in your life; and God's power will be manifested in your life.

JESUS CLAIMS TO BE LORD

Jesus told the disciples, "Ye call me Master and Lord: and ye say well; for so I am" (John 13:13). He invited men to follow him as Lord. "If any man will come after me, let him deny himself, and take up his cross daily, and follow me" (Luke 9:23). He as Lord demands loyalty. "And why call ye me, Lord, Lord, and do not the things which I say?" (Luke 6:46).

THE FULLNESS DEMANDS HIS LORDSHIP

If the Spirit would fill us, we must be abandoned and available. "No man can say that Jesus is the Lord, but by the Holy Ghost" (1 Cor. 12:3).

There was a coronation service in heaven and Jesus

was glorified. The Spirit came in mighty demonstrations of power upon the earth, the direct result of his crowning. Let his crowning take place in us, and the same Spirit will move in power.

Knowing that he is *resident* in your life, ask him to be the *reigning* Lord of your life. Have your own private coronation service and bow to him as Lord. Allow God to bring your life into line with his lordship. Let him have your business, your home, and your relationships. Say to him: "Lord Jesus, I vacate the throne of my life right now. I call you Lord, Lord of all. I give you my life, my home, my business, my pleasure, my treasure, and my plans. I ask you to do with me *as* you will, *where* you will, *when* you will. Reign without a rival in my life. Yours is the throne."

> All hail the power of Jesus' name! Let angels prostrate fall;
> Bring forth the royal diadem, and crown him Lord of all!
> Let every kindred, every tribe, On this terrestrial ball,
> To him all majesty ascribe, and crown him Lord of all!

Reckoning his death secures your salvation. Reckoning his resurrection secures his indwelling. Reckoning his *reign* secures for you the fulness of the Holy Spirit in your life. Just then, as he begins his reign in you, you will discover for the first time the release of his life.

Just today a letter came to my desk from a preacher friend who stated, "I have given my life completely to Christ for the very first time, and my ministry is completely changed." Now Jesus was beginning his public ministry in him.

Last week a letter came from a denominational worker

saying, "I learned in your service last week the meaning of dying to myself. Now I have something to say to people. Praise the Lord." Jesus was his Lord for the first time.

When the work of the Lord gives way to the Lord of the work, the work of the Lord will be wonderful.

As brief as this division is, it is the hinge upon which swings the door of triumph. The great question is, "Will you have this One to be your King?" Will you lose yourself in adoration, abandonment, and availability to him? The answer being "Yes!" will mean the life of God in Christ let loose by the power of the Holy Spirit. That, my friend, will be exciting. Let us go on.

A SERVICE OF CORONATION

"The earth is the Lord's, and the fulness thereof; the world, and they that dwell therein" (Ps. 24:1).

JESUS IS LORD!

"Wherefore God also hath highly exalted him, and given him a name which is above every name: That at the name of Jesus every knee should bow, of things in heaven, and things in earth, and things under the earth; and that every tongue should confess that Jesus Christ is Lord, to the glory of God the Father" (Phil. 2:9-11).

JESUS IS LORD!

"Ye call me Master and Lord: and ye say well; for so I am" (John 13:13). "Not everyone that saith unto me, Lord, Lord, shall enter into the kingdom of heaven; but he that doeth the will of my father which is in heaven" (Matt. 7:21).

JESUS IS LORD!

"His name shall be called Wonderful, Counsellor, The mighty God, The everlasting Father, The Prince of Peace. Of the increase of his government and peace there shall be no end. . . . The zeal of the Lord of hosts will perform this" (Isa. 9:6-7).

JESUS IS LORD!

"For none of us liveth to himself, and no man dieth to himself. For whether we live, we live unto the Lord; and whether we die, we die unto the Lord: whether we live therefore, or die, we are the Lord's. For to this end Christ both died, and rose, and revived, that he might be Lord both of the dead and living" (Rom. 14:7-9).

JESUS IS LORD!

"Lift up your heads, O ye gates; and be ye lift up, ye everlasting doors; and the King of glory shall come in. Who is this King of Glory? The Lord strong and mighty, the Lord mighty in battle. Who is this King of glory? The Lord of hosts, he is the King of glory" (Ps. 24:7-8,10).

JESUS IS LORD!

PART II
PRINCIPLES OF FULNESS

PRINCIPLES

The lordship of Christ becomes a living reality at the point of the believer's unqualified submission. Jesus is glorified in the believer as Lord at that moment. As it was in history, so it is in the individual that, when he exalts Jesus to the throne of his life, the Holy Spirit comes to fill the life. It can then be properly said that the lordship of Christ and the fulness of the Spirit are two sides of the same experience. If Jesus is Lord, we are filled with the Spirit. If we are filled with the Spirit, it is because

Jesus is Lord. The immediate work of Jesus as he begins
his reign is that of filling us with his Spirit. At this point
it is easy to confuse the person and place of the Holy
Spirit as differentiated from Jesus. In reality it is impossible to differentiate between them. It is by the Holy Spirit
that Jesus himself lives in the hearts of believers. It is
the task of the Holy Spirit to take the things of Christ
and make them known to us. Thus it soon becomes obvious that we are INDWELT, not just by one member
of the Trinity but all three. Thus, this is our first principle
with which we deal.

THE PRINCIPLE OF INDWELLING

We make a mistake in approaching the Holy Spirit if
we assume any other fact than that he comes to dwell
in every believer at conversion. Having made this mistake
we shall make another in looking to the outside for feelings and emotions instead of to the inside to spiritual
realities. We have begun the steps toward *fulness* when
we acknowledge that we are indwelt of the Holy Spirit
as well as by the Father and the Son. "Even the Spirit
of truth . . . but ye know him; for he dwelleth with
you, and shall be *in* you" (John 14:17). Jesus promised
his indwelling when he said, "At that day ye shall know
that I am in my Father, and ye in me, and I in you"
(John 14:20). He further included the Father when he
said in John 14:23, "If a man love me, he will keep my
words: and my Father will love him, and *we* will come
unto him, and make our abode with him."

As Paul wrote the church at Corinth, he used the fact
that they were indwelt by the Spirit to incite more care
regarding their bodies. He asked in 1 Corinthians 3:16,
"Know ye not that ye are the temple of God, and that
the Spirit of God dwelleth in you?" What a revelation

for the believer to consider, "The Spirit is living in me and is no less than God in Christ." Paul relates simply that, "Ye are not in the flesh, but in the Spirit, if so be that the Spirit of God dwell in you" (Rom. 8:9). Then again Paul states, "But if the Spirit of him that raised up Jesus from the dead dwell in you, he . . . shall also quicken your mortal bodies by his spirit that dwelleth in you" (Rom. 8:11). So, within three verses we are informed that we are indwelt by the "Spirit of God," the "Spirit of Christ," and the "Spirit."

As we study the principle of indwelling, we necessarily come to the consideration of the term . . . the baptism of the Spirit. Paul said of this baptism, "For by one Spirit are we all baptized into one body. . . . and have all been made to drink into one Spirit" (1 Cor. 12:13). At Pentecost the Holy Spirit came in a mighty baptism upon the church, the body of Christ. Christ had said, "But tarry ye in the city of Jerusalem, until ye be endued with power from on high" (Luke 24:49). He further said, "But ye shall receive power, after that the Holy Ghost is come upon you" (Acts 1:8). The second chapter of Acts records that mighty baptism which was a fulfilling of the promise of Mark 1:8, "I indeed have baptized you with water: but he shall baptize you with the Holy Ghost." The fourth Gospel quotes thusly, "[He] Upon whom thou shalt see the Spirit descending, and remaining on him, the same is he which baptizeth with the Holy Ghost" (John 1:33).

Thus we see that the mystic body of Christ, the church, was baptized on the day of Pentecost. As each of us becomes a member of that body, we are baptized with the same Spirit that indwells that body, and we receive the gift of the Holy Spirit. It is our *baptism* or gift of the Spirit that makes possible the *fulness* of the Spirit. It is through the baptism of the Spirit that he comes to indwell us.

THE PRINCIPLE OF CHRIST'S CAPACITIES

If I am indwelt of Christ, where is the Holy Spirit?
If I am filled with the Holy Spirit, where is Christ? Who
dwells in me, anyway? We will clarify this more than
once, for in it is one of the most vital facets of the life
of fulness. Say this to yourself at least three times: "ALL
OF GOD IS IN CHRIST; ALL OF CHRIST IN-
DWELLS ME BY THE HOLY SPIRIT; THEREFORE,
I AM INDWELT BY GOD THE FATHER, GOD THE
SON, AND GOD THE HOLY SPIRIT!" To speak of
one is to speak of all.

But let us think of it from another standpoint, namely,
of the Jesus of earth and the Jesus of heaven. The Jesus
of earth was the incarnate Son of God with human mother
and human body. The Jesus of heaven is not only at
the right hand of God exalted, but indwells every believer
by the Holy Spirit. The Jesus of earth came in humiliation
to live *among* us, *with* us, and die *for* us. The Jesus of
heaven (the Holy Spirit) is glorified and poured out in
power. The Jesus of earth was limited and could only
be one place at a time. His teaching was confined to
the slowness of the disciples to understand and believe.
For this reason he said, "I have yet many things to say
unto you, but ye cannot bear them now. Howbeit when
he, the Spirit of truth, is come he will guide you into
all truth" (John 16:12-13). The Jesus of heaven (the Holy
Spirit) is that *new* teacher who teaches from within. Someone designates the Holy Spirit simply as "the other self
of Jesus" while B. H. Carroll shortens the title to call
the Holy Spirit "the other Jesus." He is the One who
stays with his people forever. The Jesus of the earth must
go away so that the Jesus of heaven might come to stay!

From this vantage point we have in Christ a dual capac-
ity. He is the One who comes to the earth to be our

dying Savior; and He is the One who, resurrected and ascended, comes to abide in us as the indwelling Lord. It is an interesting parallel to the work of Moses, the deliverer, and Joshua, the guiding general who led Israel into the land of promise. The Israelites were brought out that they might be brought in. Moses would be the one who would be used in the "bringing out." Joshua would be the one who would be used in the "bringing in." Jesus, our Savior on earth, and our indwelling Lord from heaven, both brings us out and takes us in. Thus when we speak of the fulness of the Spirit we are inevitably speaking of the fulness of Christ.

THE PRINCIPLE OF CONFESSION AND CLEANSING

As we come to appropriate the fulness of the Spirit in our personal lives, we come immediately to be confronted with the principle of confession and cleansing. The teaching of many on the Holy Spirit is deficient because little or nothing is made of cleansing and its prerequisite, confession. When confession is complete, all hindrances are removed and the Holy Spirit responds with the fulness. This is the point at which the great revivals of the past have begun. Miss Bertha Smith, famed missionary and Spirit-filled phenomenon, testifies that in the great Shantung revival confession and cleansing characterized its central thrusts among the believers. She advocates then that "every sin must be confessed, forsaken, and all wrongs made right, that we may be cleansed." There can be no filling that is not preceded with an emptying. This self-emptying can only come as we honestly ". . . walk in the light, as he is in the light . . ." (1 John 1:7) and confess our sins for cleansing.

Ruth Paxson cites three reasons for the lack of the

fulness of the Spirit: (1) ignorance, (2) unbelief, and (3) *unconfessed* sin. Before God would bless his house in 2 Chronicles 29 he said, "Sanctify now yourselves, and sanctify the house of the Lord God of your fathers, and carry forth the filthiness out of the holy place" (v.5). For sixteen days they carried out the filthiness. Only then was God ready to bless his house.

Many a believer has been kept from the blessed fulness of the Spirit by an unconfessed sin of such little proportion, humanly speaking, that one would be apt to pass over it. The Holy Spirit cannot tolerate sin.

THE PRINCIPLE OF DEATH UNTO LIFE

We have already touched on this matter, but now we come to relate it to the fulness of the Spirit. As we identify with Christ on the cross, we reckon the death of self. Dr. A. B. Simpson writes, "The Holy Spirit is the Great Undertaker who finally brings us to the place to which God has assigned us; namely, the sharing of Christ's tomb. But he cannot bring us to participation in the crucifixion-life without our consent. We must consent to die." Thus consenting to die, we consent to the life of Jesus in us by the Holy Spirit residing and reigning. We can only be alive in him as we are dead to ourselves. This is the principle of the exchanged life. The life of the old man is reckoned dead that the life of the new man (Christ Jesus) might take its place to give victory. If we would live, we must die. It is as simple as that. This is the reason why the experience of fulness comes to most within the context of despair. It is not uncommon for one to become so miserable in the life of the flesh, even in the midst of success, that he wishes with all his heart for the privilege of dying. Only when one gets to the place where he is willing to die will God answer his prayer and teach him to do so. In a recent prayer meeting after a session of the Arkansas Baptist Pastors' Retreat, I heard one praying just behind me with much urgency, "Oh, Lord, fill me or kill me!" I quietly praised the Lord that he was in the process of doing the latter so he could do the former! I was much opposed to speaking of the fulness of the Spirit until I became so miserable I wanted to die. Men ready to die do not have near as many hang-ups as those determined to live. Accepting the lordship of Christ and thus the fulness of the Holy Spirit means nothing less than the acceptance of death to the self-life.

Jesus has proclaimed no bargain days when the entrance qualifications for discipleship have been lowered. It is still "deny yourself, take up your cross daily, and follow me" (Luke 9:23). So, if you would have his fulness, get ready to die!

THE "THIRST . . . COME . . . DRINK" PRINCIPLE

In that great declaration on the last day of the feast, Jesus cried with a loud voice, "If any man thirst, let him come unto me, and drink" (John 7:37). The steps toward fulness cannot be made any clearer than they are made here.

Thirst denotes intensity of *desire*. If one would be filled with the Spirit, he must *desire* it with all his heart. Until the desire pervades his whole being, he is not prepared for glorious fulness of the Spirit.

Coming to Jesus denotes intent of *direction*. We are to come to Jesus. If Christ *is* all and *in* all, then he *has* all we need. We can come to him knowing he, himself, is the blessed resource from which all fulness comes.

Drinking denotes participation, appropriation, and receiving. We "drink" of Jesus. It is by drinking that we are filled. Paul uses this figure in Ephesians 5:18, "Be not drunk with wine . . . but be filled with the Spirit." One gets drunk by drinking. One continues to stay drunk by continuing to drink. Peter and the others were accused of being drunk as they moved under the strange and wonderful power of the Holy Spirit. And drunk they were! They were intoxicated on the reality of the *risen, resident, reigning* Lord within their lives who was being *released* by the Spirit through their lives. Strong drink sometimes makes men very different from their former sober selves. Timid men become bold. Quiet men become vocal. Greedy men become generous. Sad, downcast men become gleeful. When a man becomes Spirit-filled, he literally becomes God-intoxicated. That marvelous change takes place within his system in which Someone besides himself takes over. The result of his labor, the figure of his countenance, and the quality of his ceaseless energy bespeak the power of God.

THE PRINCIPLE OF FAITH

I left this word out in the sequence for many years . . . "believe." After the thirst . . . come . . . drink sequel, the next words say, "He that *believeth* on me . . . out of his belly [inner man] shall flow rivers of living water" (John 7:38). Many miss the fulness of the Spirit on a technicality. They thirst, they come, they drink, and then they expect great emotion, feelings, upheavals, and physical phenomena. This is seldom the case. For many years I prayed to receive the fulness and was emotionally geared to expect convulsive weeping, emotional trauma, and feelings of ecstasy. When these would not come, I would go back again to life as usual, hoping for something to happen next time. Then there came the time when I was convinced that God wanted to fill me with his Spirit infinitely more than I could ever desire it. I included the word "believe" in the formula given by Christ in John 7:37-38 and quietly said: "Thank you, Jesus, for the fulness you promised. I feel nothing at the moment, but I do believe! I have confessed every sin of which you have convicted me. I die to myself that you might live as my Lord. I thank you very much." I had only one reason to believe that he had filled me with his Holy Spirit . . . HE SAID HE WOULD! He did! Then came the next word in the sequence . . . *flow*. This leads to our next principle.

THE PRINCIPLE OF DIVINE FLOW

In our study of how we function, we mentioned the *divine flow*. This, simply put, is the natural flow of the life of God through the human life as he intended. We were not made to be mere containers of divine life but channels of that life. As Jesus becomes our Lord, he reverses the flow of the influence of the world. We who were influenced by the world and were at the mercy of our environment and circumstances now discover that he in us is moving out through us with his life. The flow of divine life is from God to us and through us to the world. We abide in him and thus keep his commandments. "And he that keepeth his commandments dwelleth [abides] in him, and he in him" (1 John 3:24). As we continue to abide in him, the flow continues from the Father in response to our faith to abide. Toward the world around us the love that is within us continues to flow. We are experiencing the *divine flow*. We who could not muster enough love to satisfy even the slightest longings of the heart now find a *river* of love flowing through us. We who have trouble finding a peaceful moment suddenly find life breaking into a *river* of peace. We who

looked for joys like a beggar searches for crumbs find
joy flowing like a river. We who had trouble being civil
in times of pressure find now rivers of patience, goodness,
and gentleness flowing from within us. We who lacked
faith are caught now in its flood. Praise the Lord for
the divine flow! How marvelous is the figure of the river!
Let us observe some of the qualities of a river:

A river is involuntary and doesn't have to try.
  A river is unselfish and available to all wherever it
  goes.
    A river is the picture of confidence and power
    and doesn't have to babble like a brook!
      A river is consistent and keeps on keeping
      on. You never have to prod it.
        A river is a picture of constant cleans-
        ing. Cast pollution in it, and it will
        sweep it away.
          A river is a symbol of courage.
          Put obstacles in front of it,
          and it will overwhelm
          them.
            A river speaks of
            power. It runs
            factories and
            turns on lights
            all over the
            country.

You don't have to plead with a river to flow. You
can't "program" a river or stop its flow. You don't have
to map its direction. It will make its own way. "AND
OUT OF [THE INNER MAN] SHALL FLOW *RIVERS*
OF LIVING WATER. . . . THIS SPAKE HE OF THE

SPIRIT, WHICH THEY THAT BELIEVE ON HIM SHOULD RECEIVE" (John 7:38-39).

THE PRINCIPLE OF CONTINUING

The baptism of the Spirit is a *once and for all* experience by which we are immersed into Christ. The fulness of the Spirit is an event which is followed by a continuing disposition of faith. Paul's injunction, in Ephesians 5:18 literally rendered, would read, "Be ye continually always being filled with the Holy Spirit." This is in line with the *thirst . . . come . . . drink* principle. Each of these is in the present tense and could well be read: "If any man continues to thirst, let him continue to drink, and as the Scriptures say, he that continues to believe, out of his inner man will continue to flow rivers of living water." Stop thirsting and you will stop coming to Jesus. Stop coming to Jesus and you will stop drinking. Stop drinking and you will stop believing for the fulness. Stop believing for the fulness and you will stop overflowing with rivers of living water. Every one of these principles mentioned is a principle upon which we must continue to reckon.

One of the most vital principles of *continuing* is found in the old Testament story of Moses (Ex. 4). When Moses threw down his rod in response to God's command, it represented a thorough, complete, and abandoned submission to the will of God. What happened was the equivalent of an enduement of power from on high. As long as the rod was in the hand of the man, it was no more than a man's rod with a man's power. God didn't want the rod; he wanted Moses . . . all of Moses. The rod stood in the path between Moses and God. Moses threw it down and it became a snake, the true nature of uncommitted self. God commanded Moses to pick it up by the tail. He would never possess it in a primary sense. It was first to be the rod of God. God sanctified it, literally "de-selfed" it, and allowed Moses to have it "by the tail." How significant the statement that was later made thoughtfully, "And he took the ROD OF GOD in his hand." But that wasn't the end. The relationship so sealed must continue. There would be crises and victories, but the principle of the Rod of God would apply every time.

Moses and the more-than-a-million people moved out and across the land to the shore of the Red Sea. Pharaoh changed his mind and sent his army after them. Now, here is a problem that will try the best of principles. Moses tried to be brave and stood before the people to say, "Stand still and see the salvation of the Lord!" I think he must have gotten behind a rock and looked to God with a distinct "what-are-we-going-to-do?" look on his face. God had asked before, "What is in thine hand?" I really believe that he must have asked it again. Moses must have replied, "Why, Lord, it's the same rod." God must have replied, "It *was* yours . . . now it is *mine*. It could do no more than you could do; it was no stronger than you were. Now it's mine and you are mine. Moses, hold up the rod—reckon on the principle!" Moses made a sweep across the sea with the rod, and the sea opened, and they went across on dry land! What had happened? It was the man of God, sold out to God, with the rod of God in his hand! It was not Moses doing his best but God in his man baring His mighty arm!

They got across the sea and turned around and saw the armies of Pharaoh coming down the same path through the waters. "What now, Lord?" Moses must have queried. "What is that in your hand, Moses?" God again asked. "Oh, yes, the ROD!" Moses reminded himself.

"Hold it up . . . declare the principle: 'It is not by might, nor by power, but by my Spirit!, saith the Lord.' " Another wave of the rod and the sea closed and the Egyptians were no more. The principle continues.

Before long they ran out of water. What a griping crowd they were! Again Moses inquired of God in the midst of unreasoning complaints. God said, "Moses, come up ahead of the people a little way, and bring some of the elders, and, by the way, bring the ROD." God brought them to the Mount of Horeb and told Moses to strike the rock. Now remember this *was* a mere rod in the hand of Moses. It could do no more than a man could do and could strike no harder than the strength of the man whose hand held it. But it was no longer the rod of a mere man but the rod of God. It could now be used as a tool of God reflecting the very power of God. He struck the rock and out gushed a flowing river. As much as many scholars would like to explain this away, the fact of a miracle remains. The power of the miracle rests in the principle of the continuing power of God operating on continued faith.

They then found themselves in the valley of Rephidim confronted by the Amalekites. (They always come sooner or later.) But Moses seemed now to be learning the principle of *continuing*. He enjoined Joshua to fight the Amalekites in the valley while he stood on the hill with the rod of God in his hand. This would declare that by the might of the hand of God the battle would be won. The battle raged, and as long as Moses held the rod high, Joshua prevailed. But when he tired, became preoccupied or negligent, and lowered the rod, the Amalekites prevailed. The battle went back and forth, always according to the position of the rod. When the rod was up, there was victory. When the rod was down, there was defeat.

Finally Aaron and Hur caught on and came to the rescue. They propped Moses up and each stationed himself at Moses' side. The rod was held high. The Bible thoughtfully declared, "And Joshua *discomfited* Amalek in the valley of Rephidim."

Thus it is with the fulness of the Spirit that as we continue to assert our death and his life, our weakness and his power, our yieldedness and his enduement, the rivers continue to flow and the battles continue to be won.

Praise the Lord for the principle of continuing!

PART II
THE POWER OF THE SPIRIT

"For God hath not given us the spirit of fear; but of POWER. . . . (2 Tim. 1:7).

The book of Acts literally explodes with *power.* The word for power in the New Testament is the word from which we get our words "dynamo," "dynamic," and "dynamite." Jesus promised just before he ascended, "Ye shall receive power" (Acts 1:8). With every turn of the page in Acts there is an explosion of power.

What strange dynamic turned the dull, dispirited, disappointed disciples into veritable dynamos overnight? What was it that caught busy old Jerusalem in the midst of a holy feast and shook it was a tornadic power? What was it that caused three thousand people to embrace Christ with an abandoned faith in a few minutes after a simple sermon? And the preacher that preached that sermon . . . what drew him out of his pit of cowardice and gave him the courage and strength of a lion? What had transformed his personality? And what was the substance of a movement which thrived best in adversities of impossible proportions and outlived the kings who prophesied its doom?

We who have read Acts, chapter 2 know what it was! The life of the Spirit of Christ entered the body of Christ and it became at that moment a living, vital, thriving, and indestructible organism. THE HOLY SPIRIT HAD COME! The promise of Jesus was fulfilled. The heritage and inheritance of everyone who would be born into that fellowship of the Spirit is the fulness of that power which became evident in the upper room that unforgettable day. . . .

"And *suddenly*
　(It was an event in time.)
there came a sound from heaven as of a rushing, mighty wind,
　(It was *audible*.).
and it filled all the house where they were sitting.
　(Something so undeniable that it must be reckoned with.)
And there appeared unto them cloven tongues like as of fire,
　(What had been audible then became *visible*.)
And it sat upon each of them. And they were all filled with the Holy Ghost,
　(What had been audible and visible then became *experiential*.)
and began to speak with other tongues,
　(Languages.)
as the Spirit gave them utterance."
　(What had been audible, visible, and experiential then became *expressive*.)   Acts 2:2-3
AND THE POWER HAD COME!!

THE REALITY OF THE POWER

One cannot read the book of Acts and deny the power of it. It flows like a river from every chapter. The reality of the power of the Spirit is reflected not only in the dramatic and overwhelming manner of his coming but in the events which were to follow. Luke is careful to give proper credit to the Spirit, mentioning the "Holy Spirit," the "Holy Ghost," or the "Spirit" over fifty times in twenty-eight chapters. You could take the Holy Spirit out of the book of Acts, and there would not be enough excitement to make a one-column news story.

A convention preacher asked a question several years ago which shattered my life. His question was, "What are you doing in your church that you could not possibly do without the power of the Holy Spirit?" I discovered to my dismay that I not only *could* do many of the things I was doing without his power, I had *been doing* it! The reality of Spirit power was not there. What a tragedy for us to suppose that we can continue to do the work of God without the supreme dynamic of our age . . . THE HOLY SPIRIT!

The saddest observation of our whole system is that there seems to be everything evident but *power*. There are elegant edifices, educational excellence, efficiency, and enthusiasm. These are all too obvious. But power is obviously absent in most of our religious expressions. The reality of Spirit power is the greatest need of our day.

THE REASONS FOR THE POWER

A Christian leader has said, "If we could but show the world today that being commited to Christ is no tame, humdrum, sheltered monotony but indeed the greatest adventure which the human spirit could ever know, the world outside looking askance at Christianity would come crowding in to pay allegiance and we could expect the greatest revival since Pentecost." But how can we show the world the Christian adventure without the *power* evident in our lives?

We come to the reason for the enduement of power . . . the *impotence of man.* Jesus freely admitted, "The Son can do nothing of Himself." The Christ of the flesh without the indwelling life of God was impotent. The great secret of Jesus was the power of the Spirit. In Isaiah the Messiah had said, "The Spirit of the Lord God is upon me; because the Lord hath anointed me . . ." (Isa. 61:1). The only answer to the *impotency* of man is the *anointing* of God. For this reason he has given us his Spirit.

The New Testament record is that God deliberately chose those who were weak through which to demonstrate the power of his Spirit. "God hath chosen the foolish things of the world to confound the wise; and God hath chosen the weak things of the world to confound the . . . mighty" (1 Cor. 1:27). God's power shows up best in weak people. For this reason Paul was heard to say, "Most gladly therefore will I rather glory in my infirmities, that the power of Christ may rest upon me" (2 Cor. 12:9).

Secondly, there was the *impossibility of the task.* There was a world then and now which was not only unreceptive to the news of Christ but was antagonistic toward it. There was no human resource which seemed available. The trends of history have always seemed set against spiritual well-being. It was impossible that anyone in his right mind should even consider the possibility of the survival of the church, much less its success. Praise the Lord for impossibilities! It is within the framework of impossibility that God works best.

Thirdly, we see the *ingenuity of Satan.* We are at war and we have a personal adversary. He is not omniscient but he is very bright. He is not omnipresent but he is speedy. He is not omnipotent but he is deceitfully tricky. To many he is one to be avoided. We must learn that "greater is he that is in you, than he that is in the world" (1 John 4:4).

Another reason for the giving of the power of the Spirit was the *iniquity of the world.* Paul warned, "For the mystery of iniquity doth already work" (2 Thess. 2:7). We are without influence in this world of overpowering sin without the Holy Spirit.

Finally, his power is made available because of the *ineshaustibility of God's resources.* God is not weakened by the bestowing of power. The indwelling Savior has all *authority* in heaven and in earth and on this basis gives us *power.*

THE RESULTS OF THE POWER

Power always brings results. Without the power, man is left to scramble for results that are achievable by human means. Thus, he settles on a table of results that best vindicate his success in human standards. He fabricates, exaggerates, and rationalizes. But with the coming of the power of the Spirit, there are results of a different proportion.

There is an exciting verse in Acts 4:33, "And with great power gave the apostles witness of the resurrection of the Lord Jesus: and great grace was upon them all." Notice that the word *great* is used twice. The word in the Greek language is *megas.* The word has come to a new usage today. In our world of awesome destructive forces we measure the power of the atom bomb by *megatons.* One megaton is the equivalent of the explosive force of one million tons of dynamite. One day, as I thought about this, I carried this matter a little further. On July 16, 1945, there was a blinding light in the Eastern United States as the first atomic bomb ever exploded took our world by the collar and thrust it into the atomic age. On August 6, 1945 the first atomic bomb was dropped as an aggressive act of war on the city of Hiroshima, Japan. This is what happened in summary:

In the city of 500,000 there were 70,000 killed immediately. Another 70,000 were injured, many dying in the hours that followed. Multiplied thousands bore terrifying scars and disabling wounds to their death. An area covering 4.7 square miles, or over 3,000 acres, was completely leveled in the downtown area of the city. Shock or blast waves moved out from the center of the explosion at twelve and one-half miles per minute, crumbling twelve-inch walls a mile away. Heat waves of millions of degrees in intensity moved out with the speed of light, melting flesh, stone, and anything else that was in the path. Now, think of this . . . that bomb was a very small one with the explosive force of 20,000 tons of dynamite This is exactly one-fiftieth of a megaton. (We now have bombs 5,000 times as powerful as the first one!)

With this fresh illustration of power on our minds, let us read the Scripture in its literal rendering. "And with a million tons of power gave the apostles witness of the resurrection of the Lord Jesus: and a million tons of grace was upon them all." That, my friend, is *awesome* power and *awesome* grace. AND THE SPIRIT OF CHRIST IN WHOM ALL POWER IS RESIDENT IS IN OUR WORLD AND IN OUR LIVES AVAILABLE TO US EVERY MOMENT FOR HOLINESS OF LIFE AND ENDUEMENT FOR WORK.

It is unlikely that in any given city today an atomic

bomb of megaton proportion could be dropped and business go on as usual. It is just as unlikely that a Holy Spirit visitation could take place in any city, church, or individual and circumstances remain the same. There would be immediate and evident results. There is no reference in the Bible to the work of the Holy Spirit in which he is not active and mighty in power.

THE RESULTS OF THE POWER

We will observe only briefly some of the immediate results of the coming of the Holy Spirit into the world. We will come to what the Holy Spirit is doing in the world today in another chapter. All that happened began to happen in the lives of the believers. *Believers were changed!* All of a sudden they who waited had direction, intensity, and purpose. They took on the glow and conduct of another world. They acted so differently that they were accused of being drunk. They were endowed with an abandoned boldness.

Not only were believers changed, but *unbelievers were saved.* Before nightfall on the day of Pentecost there were three thousand added to their ranks! And indeed the quality of those saved in *Holy Spirit evangelism* is notable. Of them it was said:

"And they continued steadfastly in the apostles' doctrine" (Acts 2:42).

"And many wonders and signs were done by the apostles" (Acts 2:43).

"And [they] sold their possessions and goods, and parted them to all men, as every man had need. And they, continuing daily with one accord in the temple . . . did eat their meat with gladness and singleness of heart, Praising God, and having favour with all the people" (Acts 2:45-47).

The world was awestruck. We may impress the world without the power of the Spirit, but we can never amaze the world. Remarks of the response of the world were frequent in the light of the moving of the Spirit.

In Acts 2:7, "They were all amazed and marvelled . . ."

In Acts 2:12, "They were all amazed . . ."

In Acts 4:13, "When they saw the boldness of Peter and John, and perceived that they were unlearned and ignorant men, they marveled."

In Acts 5:11, "And great fear came upon all the church, and upon as many as heard these things.".

To follow the trail of the Holy Spirit is to witness his phenomenal power all the way. The tidal wave of power was to sweep toward Gaza and save the man from Ethiopia. It knocked Saul of Tarsus off his feet and filled him for service. It did not stop with Cyprus, Corinth, or Rome. It went on and is still going. After more than nineteen hundred years, the power of the Spirit is just as fresh as when he first came at Pentecost.

LIVING IN ACTS "TWENTY-NINE"

The story is not finished! The last chapter is being written . . . we are living in Acts 29! There is no reason to be given under heaven why this last chapter should not be the most exciting chapter of all. There is every reason to expect that as the people of God beseech God for revival, there will be a mighty Holy Spirit visitation across the land.

I have read of the Puritan revival which occurred when the Bible was given in the language of the people. Copies of the Bible, being scarce, were placed in the entrances of a few churches. People from miles around would come to hear just the reading of the Word and a mighty revival touched off. My response is . . . *Lord, do it again!*

I have heard of the New England Awakening under Jonathan Edwards when God's mighty presence filled the city of Northampton. In the early months of 1735 thousands pressed into the church daily to pray and worship. Taverns were emptied, and men paused in the streets in the daytime and at night to talk together about the love of Jesus. The result of that revival was that almost the whole adult population of the city was saved. Ministers from other places would come and visit and carry word of revival back to their congregations where it would happen again!

Word has been written of the revivals under the Wesleys, Whitfield, and Brainerd. In the nineteenth century it was Charles Grandison Finney that was to be the firebrand of revival. In one region during that revival over 5,000 people were saved without a single minister settled in that area. Dr. Lyman Beecher said, "This is the greatest work of God and the greatest revival of religion that the world has ever seen in so short a time." My prayer is . . . *"Lord, do it again!"*

I read the history of the revival in Wales near the turn of the century. God heard the prayer of an aging saint, Seth Joshua, who prayed: "God send a revival to Wales. Don't send us somebody from Oxford to preach to our pride or somebody from Cambridge to preach to our intellect. Touch some little lad in the mining regions and raise him up for revival." As Joshua was praying that prayer, God was readying a little lad name Evan Roberts. In the fulness of time the Spirit of power swept through Wales and thousands of people were saved. Over five hundred ministers of the gospel were saved in the awakening.

There were others in the Hebrides, in Scotland, and

in China. But sadly enough, the last great revival of notice-able proportions in America took place in 1857! No fa-mous men are connected with this revival. It just seemed to happen spontaneously in answer to the combined pray-ers of millions of saints across the sad and sickened land. As the revival came, miracles were too numerous to men-tion. Whitehaired penitents knelt with little children to receive Chirst as Savior. Whole families of Jews were converted to faith in the Messiah. Deaf mutes responded to the power and became so filled with power that, though they could not speak a word, they were among the most effective of witnesses through the glow of countenance. Hardened infidels were melted and were led down the aisles by little children. Ships in the harbor would become the scenes of revival outbreaks. Many ships reported as they passed to within sight of land that the Holy Spirit seized all on board and brought them to their knees in genuine repentance and faith. It is estimated that in the height of the revival season over fifty thousand people a week came to saving faith. I say, *"Lord, do it again!"*

In 1970 in the little college town of Wilmore, Kentucky, God moved into a college chapel service in the power of his spirit and lengthened the fifty-minute chapel service to one hundred and eighty hours of continuous revival. More than twenty news media personnel were saved as they visited to cover the phenomenon. I visited and preached in that chapel a few months after revival broke out. The presence of the Almighty hovered over that little town with unmistakable glory. And it goes on!

I think I hear the muffled tones of weeping on the part of millions in spiritual hunger and the not-so-muffled tones of our Lord calling us back to our first love. I believe that we are hearing the "sound of a going in the tops of the mulberry trees," signifying that God is begin-

ning his last mighty visitation on this earth before Christ
comes. We are witnessing the first mighty winds of this
visitation. This is Acts 29!

Come, Holy Spirit, Heavenly Dove,
   With all Thy quickening powers,
Kindle a flame of sacred love
   In these cold hearts of ours.

Lord, as of old at Pentecost Thou didst Thy power
display,
   With cleansing, purifying flame, descend on us today!
Lord, send the old-time power, the Pentecostal
power!
   Thy floodgates of blessing on us throw open wide!
Lord, send the old-time power, the Pentecostal
power,
   That sinners be converted and Thy name glorified!

My prayer has changed. I need no longer pray, "Lord,
do it again." The Lord *is* doing it again! My prayer is,
"Lord, let it go on until Jesus comes!"

PART II
IS THERE A SECOND BLESSING?

I remember from my earliest childhood hearing of the
term "second work of grace" or "second blessing." There
were those who believed that salvation was not enough
and that, as soon as one came to know Christ as Savior,
he should begin to seek that "second blessing." I watched
person after person plead for this experience in his life
without avail. My grandfather, one of the godliest men
I ever knew, sought for this experience during the days

of my knowledge of him. He never received it and mourned the fact that he had not until he died. He was as committed to Christ and as intimate with him as any man I had ever known. He could not pray without weeping, even in brief prayers of thanks at the meal table. Yet, he died mourning the fact that he had not felt certain emotions and experienced certain manifestations that made up what he called "the second blessing."

Is there a "second blessing?" A usual and correct answer to that question is, "There certainly is . . . and a third and a fourth and a fifth and a million more." This does not, however, settle the issue. Every now and then someone will come to me after a sermon on the Holy Spirit and say, "I am so glad to find a Baptist who is a 'second blessing' preacher." My immediate reply is usually, "The fulness of the Holy Spirit is not a second blessing, but rather the SECOND HALF OF THE FIRST BLESSING." When Jesus Christ came into my heart, it was by the Holy Spirit. It is by the Holy Spirit that he abides there now. It is by the Holy Spirit that we can all be filled continuously with the life of Jesus. The entire work of grace embraces Christ coming to abide, abiding to fill, and continuing to overflow. This work of grace is not meted out over a period of time according to the believer's conduct, sacrifice, or worthiness.. At the moment of salvation Christ comes into the life. The Father dwells in the Son, thus the Father comes into the life. This is all the work of the Holy Spirit. Thus, it can properly be said that the Father dwells in us in Christ by the Holy Spirit. He has then, with Christ, ". . . freely given us all things" (Rom. 8:32).

Now, from that point on, the Christian life is a matter of appropriating what we already possess. Paul said, "Therefore let no man glory in men. FOR ALL THINGS

ARE YOURS" (1 Cor. 3:21). It is much the same as receiving a large sum of money in the form of a deposit receipt. You know the name of the bank, the person making the deposit; and you have a checkbook to use to appropriate it as you need it. It is daily faith that causes you to reckon on the fact that the money is in the bank awaiting your needs. Thus, you continue to draw on it according to your needs. For this reason Paul affirmed, "My God shall supply all your needs according to his riches in glory by Christ Jesus" (Phil. 4:19).

But there is in the lives of most of those whom God is able to use to any great degree an experience subsequent to the conversion experience which is looked upon as a turning point in their lives. Whatever it is called, it is of such nature that their lives will never be the same. The experience of Saul of Tarsus bears this out when, subsequent to his conversion on the road to Damascus, he came to Ananias, who said, "Brother Saul, the Lord, even Jesus, that appeared unto thee in the way as thou camest, hath sent me, that thou mightest receive thy sight, and *be filled with the Holy Ghost*" (Acts 9:17). Paul had met the Lord Jesus on the road to Damascus; in this city he was filled with the Spirit.

There is no more dramatic a change than that which took place in the life of Peter between the narratives in Matthew 26 and Acts 2. In Matthew 26 we find a fearful disciple, cowering before a little girl. His sin became progressively worse until, in hot words of anger, he recalled some of the language from his old life and began to swear, saying, "I know not the man." Then, when the cock crew, Peter remembered the words of Jesus and went out to weep bitterly. He was defeated, disappointed, and dejected, but he was not through! It was that same Peter, the coward, who was filled with the Spirit, who preached that sermon in Jerusalem to which about three thousand people responded in coming to Christ.

Down through the years of history men who have been saved have given an account of a time in their lives when something so mighty happened that they were never the same again.

We don't do well today in turning our minds from such a dynamic as the Holy Spirit. Nor do we well in discounting the fact of the necessity of an experience in which one is filled with the Spirit of power. If you consider this to be a controversial doctrine, consider also the fact that men such as Spurgeon, Finney, Moody, Torrey, Sunday, Scarborough, and others believed in the fulness of the Holy Spirit and the enduement of power from on high.

Perhaps the movements in the world that emphasize gifts and manifestations more than the Holy Spirit himelf present us one of our gravest problems. We can make one of two mistakes in reacting to such movements. We can *fight* them or *flee* them. Either course would be the choice of the devil for us. What we should be determined to do is to pursue our course of seeking the fulness of God in the manner in which he desires to give it. The simple fact remains that when we make all that we are his, something happens! That something, regardless of what it may be called, results in the abundant life that Jesus promised to all that are his. Let every Christian who resides anywhere on the short side of victory be quick to know that there is *more, much more* and that this *much more* can be appropriated as the Holy Spirit is allowed to take over our lives completely.

It is well that we view some of the men in times past in whose lives this experience of the Spirit's fulness came to be real.

Dwight L. Moody

The son of Mr. Moody, in writing the life story of his father, stated that there was a crucial year in the life of this famous preacher. During the year of 1871 he became more and more aware of how little he was fitted for his work. An intense hunger and thirst for spiritual power was aroused in him by two women who would attend the meetings and sit on the front seat. He could see by their expressions that they were praying. At the close of the services they would say to him:

"We have been praying for you."

"Why don't you pray for the people?" Mr. Moody would ask.

"Because *you* need the power of the Spirit," they would say.

"I need the power? Why," said Mr. Moody, in relating the incident years later, "I thought I had the power. I had the largest congregations in Chicago, and there were many conversions. I was in a sense satisfied. But right along those two godly women kept praying for me, and their earnest talk about anointing for special service set me to thinking. I asked them to come and talk with me, and they poured out their hears in prayer tht I might receive the filling of the Holy Spirit. There came a great hunger into my soul. I did not know what it was. I began to cry out as I never did before. I really felt that I did not want to live if I could not have this power for service."

Then the Chicago fire came and Moody became involved in the work of raising funds for the building of the northside tabernacle. During a trip East the hunger for more spiritual power seized him again.

"My heart was not in the work of begging," he said. "I could not appeal. I was crying all the time that God would fill me with his Spirit. Well, one day, in the city of New York . . . oh, what a day! . . . I cannot describe it, I seldom refer to it, it is almost too sacred an experience for me to name. Paul had an experience of which he never spoke for fourteen years. I can only say that God revealed himself to me, and I had such an experience of his love that I had to ask him to stay his hand. I went to preaching again. The sermons were not different; I did not present any new truths, and yet hundreds were converted. I would not now be placed back where I was before that blessed experience if you should give me all the world . . . it would be as small as dust in the balance."[12]

When R. A. Torrey presented his message entitled, "Why God Used D. L. Moody," he named several qualities which were evident in the reasons for his usefulness. The last one named, and the most important, was, "Moody was definitely endued with power from on high." Torrey further described the experience of Moody:

"Mr. Moody was walking up Wall Street in New York, and, in the midst of the bustle and hurry, his prayer for fulness was suddenly answered; the power of God fell upon him and he had to hurry to the home of a friend and ask that he might have a room by himself. In that room he stayed alone for hours; and the Holy Ghost came upon him filling his soul with such joy that at last he asked God to stay his hand lest he die on the spot from the very joy. He went out from that place with the power of the Holy Ghost upon his life."

J. Wilbur Chapman

Dr. Chapman tells how he went before God and consecrated himself and then said in faith, "My Father, I now claim from Thee the infilling of the Holy Ghost," and he said: "From that moment to this, he has been a living reality. I never knew what it was to love my family before.

I never knew what it was to study the Bible before. And why should I, for had I not just then found the key? I never knew what it was to preach before. 'Old things have passed away' in my experience. 'Behold all things have become new.' "

Oswald Chambers

Mr. Chambers was one of the mightiest men of God who ever lived. But there was a time when he was a thirsty, hungry Christian and struggled with deep inner desires. He said:

"The Holy Spirit must anoint me for the work, fire me, and so vividly convince me that such and such a way is mine to aim at, or I shall not go, I will not, I dare not, I shall not be content to earn my living. From my childhood the persuasion has been of a work, strange and great, and experience deep and peculiar. It has haunted me ever and ever. Here is the lamb and the wood but where is the fire? Nothing but the fire of the Holy Spirit can make the offering holy and unblameable in his sight."

During that time of misery he wrote the following lines:

"Let me climb, let me climb, I'm sure I've time
Ere the mist comes up from the sea,
Let me climb in time to the height sublime,
Let me reach where I long to be!"

He heard Dr. F. B. Meyer speak on the Holy Spirit. It was there that he asked God for all he had. But for four years Mr. Chambers had no conscious communion with God and found motives questionable. The Bible to him was dull and uninteresting. Then there came the time when he claimed Luke 11:13 as his own. "If ye then, being evil, know how to give good gifts unto your children: how much more shall your heavenly Father give the Holy Spirit to them that ask him?"

In a meeting shortly after this he stood and said that he must prove this verse to himself. A lady worker said, "Very good, brother, you have spoken for the rest of us." He got up again and said, "I spoke for none of you. I got up for my own sake. Either Christianity is a fraud or I have not got hold of the right end of the stick." Then and there he claimed what God had for him on the basis of that Scripture referred to before.

In describing that experience he said:

"I had no vision of heaven or angels. I had nothing . . . no power or realization of God, no witness of the Spirit. Then I was asked to speak at a meeting and forty people came to Christ. Did I praise God? No! I was terrified and left the meeting. A friend said, 'Don't you remember claiming the gift of the Holy Spirit?' Then like a flash, something happened inside me, and I saw that I had been wanting power in my own hand, so to speak, that I might say, 'Look what I have by putting my all on the altar.' I was filled with the love of God. By faith we receive the fulness just as by faith we received Christ. It is no wonder that I should talk so much about an altered disposition. God altered mine; I was there when he did it."[13]

R. A Torrey

Dr. Torrey, in his own book, *The Holy Spirit, Who He Is and What He Does,* describes the coming of the Spirit of power upon him:

"I recall the exact spot where I was kneeling in prayer in my study. It was a quiet moment, one of the most quiet moments I ever knew. Then God simply said to me, not in any audible voice, but in my heart, 'It's yours. Now go and preach.' He had already said it to me in his Word in 1 John 5:14-15; but I did not know my

Bible as I know it now, and God had pity on my ignorance and said it directly to my soul. I went and preached, and I have been a new minister from that day to this. Sometime after this experience (I do not recall just how long after), while sitting in my room one day, suddenly, I found myself shouting (I was not brought up to shout and I am not of a shouting temperament, but I shouted like the loudest, shouting Methodist), 'Glory to God, glory to God, glory to God,' and I could not stop. But that was not when I was baptized with the Holy Spirit. I was baptized with the Holy Spirit when I took him by simple faith in the Word of God."

You will notice that Torrey spoke of the experience of "baptism," as did some of the other great men of Christian history. Though we do not agree with the term, we should not be so disturbed as to turn from the need of a positive experience of fulness for ourselves. In fact, I had rather see a man who had the *fulness* and called it the *baptism,* than one who called it the *fulness* and had *nothing.*

Charles G. Finney

Mr. Finney was another who used the term "baptism of the Spirit." Though we do not use that same term for this experience, we praise the Lord in the knowledge that the hand of God was mighty upon his life and ministry. In his autobiography he tells of his experience:

"I was converted to God on the morning of the 10th of October, 1821. In the evening of the same day I received the overwhelming baptism of the Holy Ghost that went through me, as it seemed to me, body and soul. I immediately found myself endued with such power from on high that a few words dropped here and there to individuals were the means of immediate conversion. My words seemed to fasten like barbed arrows in the souls of men.

They cut like a sword. They broke the heart like a hammer. Multitudes can attest to this. Oftentimes a word dropped without my remembering it would fasten conviction and often result in almost immediate conversion. Sometimes I would find myself, in a great measure, empty of this power. I would go and visit and find that I made no saving impression. I would exhort and pray, with the same result. I would then set apart a day for private fasting and prayer, fearing that this power had departed from me, and would inquire anxiously after the reason for this apparent emptiness. After humbling myself and crying out for help, the power would return to me with all its freshness. This has been the experience of my life. This power is a great marvel. I have many times seen people unable to endure the Word. This power seems sometimes to pervade the atmosphere of the one who is highly charged with it. Many times great numbers of persons in a community will be clothed with this power when the very atmosphere of the whole place seems charged with the life of God. Strangers coming into and passing through the place will be instantly smitten with conviction of sin and in many instances converted to Christ. When Christians humble themselves and consecrate their all afresh to Christ and ask for this power, they will often receive such a baptism that they will be instrumental in converting more souls in one day than in all their lifetime before. While Christians remain humble enough to retain this power, the work of conversion will go on, till whole communities and regions of the country are converted to Christ. The same is true of the ministry."[14]

Evan Roberts

Evan Roberts was greatly used of God in the famous Welch Revival early in this century. In sharing his own experience, Mr. Roberts writes, "For thirteen years I had prayed for the Spirit. I said to myself, 'I will have the Spirit.' Through every kind of weather and in spite of all difficulties, I went to the meetings for prayer for revival. It was the Spirit that moved me thus. In one of the meetings the evangelist was praying for the Lord to 'bend us.' " The Spirit seemed to speak to Mr. Roberts, "That's what you need, to be bent." Then he tells what happened:

"I felt a living force within my bosom. This grew and grew, and I was almost bursting. My bosom was boiling. What boiled within me was the verse: 'God commending his love.' I fell on my knees with my arms over the seat in front of me; the tears and perspiration flowed freely. I thought blood was gushing forth. My prayer was 'Lord, bend me! Bend me!' After I was bent, a wave of peace came over me, and the audience sang, 'I hear Thy welcome voice.' And as they sang I thought about the bending at the Judgment Day, and I was filled with compassion for those that would have to bend on that day, and I wept. Henceforth, the salvation of souls became the burden of my heart. From that time I was set fire with a desire to go through all Wales, and, if it were possible, I was willing to pay God for the privilege of going."[15]

Evan Roberts was the key figure in one of the greatest Spirit visitations in the history of Christianity, as the whole of the little country of Wales was caught up in the spiritual adventure.

Charles Trumbull

Mr. Trumbull was for many years the editor of the *Sunday School Times.* He tells the story of his renewal in the book, *Victory in Christ:*

"We read about a certain man who had been thirty and eight years in his infirmity, and of whom Jesus asked the question, 'Wouldest thou be made whole.' And then to whom a moment later, Jesus said, 'Arise and walk. And straightway the man was made whole . . . and he arose and walked.

"This passage means a great deal to me. For I knew another man who for thirty and eight years was in the infirmity of spiritual paralysis through his bondage to sin, and who longed to be made whole; and to whom our Lord one day said, 'Arise and walk.' I was a boy about thirteen when I first made public confession of Jesus Christ as my personal Saviour; but it was not until twenty-five years later that I even knew that Christ offered to anyone in this life the power that he does offer for victory over sin. And I am convinced that many Christians, sincere, regenerated, born–again believers in the Lord Jesus Christ as their personal Saviour, are in bondage and paralysis because, like myself, they have not known of our Lord's wonderful offer. They are paralyzed, as I was, by the mistake of thinking that we ourselves must share in doing that which God alone can do.

"The conscious needs of my life, before there came that new experience of Christ of which I would tell you, were definite enough. Three stand out:

1. There were great fluctuations in my spiritual life, in my conscious closeness of fellowship with God. Sometimes I would be on the heights spiritually; and sometimes I would be in the depths. I would stay up for a while but it wouldn't last. It seemed to me that it ought to be possible for me to live habitually on a high plane of close fellowship with God, as I saw certain other men doing. Those men were exceptional to be sure; they were in the minority among the Christains whom I knew. But I wanted to be in that minority. Why shouldn't we all be, and turn it into a majority?

2. Another conscious lack of my life was in the matter of failure before besetting sins. I was not fighting a winning fight in certain lines. I had prayed, oh, so earnestly, for deliverance; and the habitual deliverance did not come.

3. A third conscious lack was in the matter of dynamic, convincing spiritual power that would work miracle changes in other men's lives."

After much time and many exposures to spiritual giants of his day, the hunger drove him to pray it out with God. Of this experience he writes,

"If there was a conception of Christ that I did not have, and that I needed because it was the secret of some of those other lives I had seen or heard of, a conception greater than any I had yet had, and beyond me, I asked God to give it to me. And God, in his longsuffering patience, forgiveness and love, gave me what I asked for. He gave me a new Christ . . . wholly new in the conception and consciousness of Christ that now became mine. Wherein is the change? It is hard to put into words, and yet it is, oh, so new and real and wonderful and miracle-working in both my own life and the life of others."[16]

In this testimony Mr. Trumbull did not even use the term, "Holy Spirit," but it is obvious that the Holy Spirit brought him to his fulness in that moment.

Frances Ridley Havergal

This song writer and author briefly tells of her experience: "It was December 2, 1873, that I first saw the blessedness of true consecration. I saw it in the flash of an electric light, and what you see you never unsee. I just utterly trusted myself to him and utterly trusted him to keep me." From that time on, life for Frances Ridley Havergal was different . . . the Holy Spirit had taken control.

Andrew Murray

For Mr. Murray there were two stages of the Christian life. He reports,

"I spent the first ten years of my Christian life in the lower stage. I was saved and could well remember the time and where. But there was no power in my service. Everything troubled me. BUT THEN THE ALMIGHTY TOOK OVER. There was no fruitfulness . . . but then Andrew Murray decided to take his place in the vine. There was no satisfaction, but he then learned that the holy One satisfieth the longing soul and filleth the hungry with goodness."

John Hyde

Mr. Hyde was on his way to the mission field in India. He was reading a letter from a friend. In that letter the friend had asked the question regarding his experience of being filled with the Spirit. He angrily crumpled the paper in his hand and threw it on the deck on the steamer. He was insulted by the fact that his friend would dare to question his consecration. Was he not going out as a missionary? Was he not a college and seminary graduate? But insult soon turned to conviction, and John Hyde went to his knees seeking the enduement of power from on high. He received it! It will never be revealed this side of heaven how many souls were turned to Christ by John Hyde, known to the Christian world as "Praying Hyde."

Stephen Merritt

A young African whose name was Kaboo had come all the way from Africa to New York to learn about the Holy Spirit from Stephen Merritt, a pastor in that city. Young Kaboo had been given the name of Samuel Morris by the missionaries who instructed him in the faith. He learned to "talk to his Father" and settle all his affairs on the basis of blind faith and nothing else. Many miracles and a very hungry heart led him to New York where he met Stephen Merritt with the words, "I am Samuel Morris. I have just come from Africa to talk with you about the Holy Ghost."

One morning Mr. Merritt went to conduct the funeral of a very prominent man in Harlem. He took Sammy Morris along with him. Other ministers were picked up along the way and expressed shock and embarrassment at having to ride with the little ragged black boy. In the midst of the ride the little black boy asked, "Did you ever pray while riding in a coach?" Merritt's answer was that he had frequently had blessed times while riding along in a coach but that he had never engaged in formal prayers. Sammy said, "We will pray." They knelt in the coach to pray and the little boy from dark Africa began to pray, "Father, I have been months in coming to see Stephen Merritt so that I could talk to him about the Holy Ghost. Now that I am here, he shows me the harbor, the churches, the banks and other buildings, but does not say a word about this Spirit that I am so anxious to hear about. Fill him with thyself so that he will not think, or talk, or write, or preach about anything but thee and the Holy Ghost."[17]

What happened in that coach was a miracle. Stephen Merritt had never experienced the burning Presence of the Holy Spirit as he did that day. He was filled with the Spirit and his whole life was changed in that amazing moment.

Time would fail to tell of hundreds of others. There seem to have been times when men did not seek this dynamic and thus Christianity went into spiritual declension. We do well to look to these lives long enough to recognize the need of the same dynamic in our day. Vital spiritual statistics seem to be declining. Skepticism and complacency reign as king and prime minister!

Dare we seek an experience of enduement of power from on high in these days? Or should we continue to reevaluate, reassess, retreat, reappoint new committees, and realign the structure? Are we ready to admit that the structure, regardless of how perfect its organization and efficient its personnel, must have the power of God upon it or be a reproach? I say that we dare do no other thing than seek God and his Spirit of power, claim his forgiveness for trusting in our own "horses and chariots," and claim personally the fulness of the Holy Spirit in our lives. We dare do no other thing!

God, grant that we hear the "sound of a going in the tops of the mulberry trees" so that when we go out we will go in the power of the Spirit of God.

PART III
THE *RELEASE* OF CHRIST *THROUGH* THE HUMAN LIFE

"That the life also of Jesus might be manifest in
our body"
2 Corinthians 4:10

"I AM COMPLETE IN HIM"
Colossians 2:10
"And wouldst thou know the secret of constant victory?
Let in the Overcomer, and he will conquer thee!
Thy broken spirit taken in sweet captivity,
Shall glory in his triumph and share his victory."

FREDA HANBURY ALLEN

TWELVE THRILLING TESTIMONIES FROM TODAY

The person with a personal testimony is never at the mercy of a person with an argument. The response of the man who had been blind was such that it hushed the argument regarding Jesus. "one thing I know, that, whereas I was blind, now I see" (John 9:25).

In these days of a fresh and vital moving of the Holy Spirit, there are hundreds of testimonies of new spiritual victories. No two testimonies are the same. The individuality of God's dealing with his own has ever been the nature of his work.

The witnesses given on the following pages are from the lives of a few who have come to a turning point, a dead end, to discover the secret. You will readily notice two things about these testimonies: first, their points of sameness; and, second, their points of difference.

In each of them I see *failure in the flesh*. It seems that we all have to come to be decisively impressed with the futility of the flesh as was Paul. He said, "For I know that in me (that is, in my flesh,) dwelleth no good thing" (Rom. 7:18).

I also see desperate desire. If the discovery of the Spirit-controlled life or the Spirit-filled life is not made shortly after conversion there is dangerous and damaging mislearning. Desperation generally must be brought about before the cycle of mislearning can be broken.

Finally, I see *thrilling triumph*. There was a difference in the life! There was a new-found joy! You will find yourself rejoicing as you read their testimonies.

As to differences, there are many. No two people came in the same manner to see their need. Some were brought to failure; others were ushered to despair on the arm of monotony. Still others were simply possessed by a sense of frustration. Some wept while others felt no emotion. Some had a traumatic emotional experience while others seemed to experience a growth process. The results are different as personalities are different.

I believe that you will benefit from reading these reports of the recent working of God in these lives.

C. B. Hogue, Evangelism Secretary of the Oklahoma Baptist Convention, shares his story:

"I gave myself to the driving goals of the ministry, often at the expense of my family, with time too short with much to be done. Five years in one pastorate and six years in another proved successful by most standards in growth, in attendance, and baptisms. The next church was geared to success, but was on its way down. All my accumulated know-how was used, but to no avail. Suddenly I was no longer successful by my standards. I gave it all I had and was ready to 'throw in the towel.' Everything I had been was emptiness.

"Through two missionaries, one from China, the other from Africa, I learned that I had been serving the cause of Christ rather than Christ himself. In agonizing misery, I came to God through reflection and searching. As I poured myself out before him, he paraded *me* before *myself.* What I saw I did not like. The experience was like a woman turning her purse up and pouring out all the contents, shaking it fiercely to see that nothing remained. I lay prostrate before God and waited for him to pour into me what he wished . . and he did! The Holy Spirit took control, immersing me in peace and joy. The room glowed with his presence. It has not been the same since. My conversion and call have a new meaning. God worked anew in my life, my church, and my family. He was in control. Joy continues to flow as I continue to drink at that fountain, knowing always every day is really sweeter than the day before."

L. Jack Gray, Missions Professor, Southwestern Baptist Theological Seminary, Fort Worth, Texas, gives his witness:

"Late Monday afternoon, March 14, 1970 in Scarborough Preaching Chapel at Southwestern Seminary, God began the most profound encounter of my life. God began to search us to the marrow of our bones making us see ourselves in shattering honesty and himself in awesome reality. God used the testimonies and confessions to bring me into the deepest conviction of sin and personal need. There settled over me a heavy demand of God that I let him set straight all strained relationships and clean out all sin. As persistently as he called me to see my guilt, he even more graciously offered heavenly cleansing, complete forgiveness, and loving acceptance.

"Having brought me very low and emptied me through the miracle of his purging, and having staggered my mind with the glory of his presence among us, he began the long task of rebuilding and filling my heart and mind with the fulness of his Spirit. This was a slow and difficult journey for me (and is still going on) because for nearly forty years I had given only fleeting attention to the clear New Testament teaching that the living Lord indwells all Christians in the person of his Holy Spirit from the day of their conversion. The reality of the sovereign Lord indwelling me had not been possessed. The comfort of his constant presence, the wisdom of his ready counsel, the flood of his unconditional love, the joy of his given

victories, and the peace that does indeed pass all understanding have begun to well up within me and overflow
'according to his riches in glory by Christ Jesus.' What
I had tried by rededication and resolution now came about
in an affirmation of faith. He showed that new birth and
daily growth are both by grace through faith.

"In the months that have followed, I have been walking
in new awareness of the presence of God as the living
Lord and have also had some awesome and devastating
encounters with Satan. But it really is true that he that
is in me is greater than he that is in the world. Meeting
Satan, problems, issues, and opportunities by faith in the
sufficiency of the Lord is becoming an orderly way of
living in the Spirit. The Word of God is becoming alive
and great hymns are becoming personal testimonies. I
am experiencing the great difference in knowing *what* I
believe and *whom* I believe! Jesus is Lord. There are 'halle-
lujahs' ringing in my soul."

Joe Ann Shelton, "Baptist Hour" soloist and musician,
Fort Worth, Texas, gives her thrilling testimony:

"I was saved at nine, but not until twenty-nine years
later did I come to see the meaning of the lordship of
Christ in my life. I listened to a preacher talk about the
inner life, and God took his words and ignited them in
my heart. He said, 'The carnal Christian is one who is
a professing Christian but has left self on the throne of
his life. The spiritual Christian has crucified self, and
Christ is on the throne.' Simple words they were, yet
profound when the Holy Spirit is teacher.

"I looked at the drawing labeled *carnal Christian* and
said, 'That's Joe Ann Shelton!' Two things took place that
night on my knees, by my bed. First, I ceased to resist
and prayed this prayer, 'Lord Jesus, I want you to be
the center of my whole being. Holy Spirit, I know you

indwell me, because at the age of nine you baptized me into the family of our Lord, but I want you now to control my life entirely.' Second, I got up from my knees believing in faith it had been done.

"Four immediate hungers and desires became evident to me. (1) Like most Christians I read my daily Bible readings when it was convenient, but now the Holy Spirit has generated within me an unquenchable thirst for the Word of God; (2) my prayer life took a drastic change for the better; (3) being a singer I thought personal soul-winning was for other folks, but how wrong I was and what a glorious discovery, and (4) I now have a new love for my church, its program, and the part I can play.

"Life has not been the same since. For twenty-nine years I had the first part of John 10:10, 'I am come that they might have life.' But now I am experiencing the 'abundant' part. All the time I had been doing things for the Lord, really working at it, not realizing that Christ wanted to *live through me*. To him be all glory and praise for his master plan of salvation through Christ Jesus."

Frank Hamby, Pastor, Bellaire Baptist Church, San Antonio, Texas, thrilled me with this testimony, "I knew the *words* for years, but I didn't have the *music!*" He spoke of the Spirit-filled life. Here is his witness:

" 'I had rather die than continue living in this hell!' These words shocked my wife that night as I faced a ministry and life that was empty and defeated. The Holy Spirit alone was able to penetrate my depression. I saw my wife transformed by the Spirit. The same thing happened in a staff member and his wife. I saw the difference in their joy and my dirge.

"Alone on a Sunday morning at the altar of the Lord, I received what I wanted—my death! As the Holy Spirit, who had lived within me all those years, now took control, my reaction was deep assurance and peace. How delicious has been the victory!"

Richard Hogue, evangelist, in his early twenties, is being mightily used of the Lord. He shares this testimony:

"I suppose it was because no one had ever fully and practically explained it to me, that the pieces had never fallen into place before. I knew that I was saved at the age of nine. I knew God had blessed my ministry in an unbelievable way. I was never so foolish to think that I could go into the pulpit without the power of the Holy Spirit. But the practical application of the fulness of the Spirit in the heart was missing in my life and I knew it. Outside the pulpit I would strive in frustration of the flesh most of the time.

"I had heard over and over in vague terms what it was that I lacked, and thought that I had tried it. The latter part of 1970 was a crisis for our team. There were problems in personal understanding as well as finances. I had heard of what the Holy Spirit was doing in the church and ministry of the author of this book and called on him to meet with my whole team. We met in December of 1970, and he shared with us what it meant to be filled with the Spirit. It was that night that our longing and thirsting came to a satisfying climax. Our whole team came to a real filling of the Spirit. What I had been afraid of was so wonderful! What a glorious difference in the attitude of the team members toward each other; in our individual spiritual lives as we witness, pray, and study the Scriptures; in my marriage; in the finances of the organization; and in the power to wage spiritual war. Most evident of all the blessings is the power of the Holy Spirit upon the invitation as we extend it night after night in the crusades.

"Without a doubt, the Holy Spirit has brought about a spiritual revolution in our team!"

Roy Fish, Professor of Evangelism, Southwestern Baptist Theological Seminary, Fort Worth, Texas, gives his joyful story:

"Many times it takes a crisis to show us our terrible inadequacy and desperate need of the Spirit's continuing fulness and control. This happened in my life some time ago when I was engaged in a week of evangelistic services. I was physically exhausted, mentally burdened, emotionally washed out, and spiritually dry. Services the first Sunday confirmed the fact that I was simply not up to it. Instead of being anxious to be used to minister to others, my anxiety was whether or not I would be able to hold myself together for eight strenuous days.

"The crisis drove me to my Lord that first Sunday evening. In the time alone with him, I took every minute detail of my life and placed it in his hands. I died that night. I died to everything in life except what he had in his plan for me. Every interest in my life I yielded to him and his will for that particular interest. I gave him my wife and family. I gave him my preaching, my sermons, that particular week of my ministry, and my depleted condition. I placed everything in the casket except what he wanted for me. Permitting my life to be his in a way I had never done before, I claimed his complete control of my life. I trusted him for his fulness.

"For the first time in weeks, I slept through an entire night. I awoke the next morning to a new liberty, exciting joy, and hitherto unknown power for service. Both from the pulpit and in personal witness there was a difference. Experientially, God confirmed to me his promise, 'Ye shall receive power after that the Holy Spirit has come upon you.' "

Steve O'Kelly is a graduate student at Southwestern Baptist Theological Seminary. God has peculiarly touched his life. He tells about it here:

"At eighteen I had a love for Jesus Christ but something was missing. I had too many spiritual ups and downs with too much dependence on feelings. One Saturday afternoon I was caught up in great conviction and confessed every known sin in my life. I told God that I was giving up. This was the significant beginning of a new walk.

"In 1970 as revival began to be experienced among some seminary students I was seized with conviction over the condition of my life. I had to confess to a professor and to my church family that I had not been letting Jesus be Lord like I had at other times. I had to write some letters and go to some friends and make things right with them. I had hesitated to commit all to Christ again for fear of failing the Lord because of a major weakness in my life. I heard an Asbury Seminary student say, 'The will of God is now. Deal with tomorrow when it becomes now.' The truth led me to new freedom and I let go of myself. Today I walk on a new basis of adventurous surrender to his best will hour by hour. I am joyously experiencing revival in my life and church."

James Ballard is pastor of the Main Street Baptist Church in Hendersonville, North Carolina. He shares the story of his breakthrough here:

"Since my conversion at the age of eleven I have known of the presence and indwelling of the Holy Spirit, but it was not until several years ago that I knew of the Spirit-filled life.

"A few years ago I contemplated leaving the ministry, for I was fed up with the shallowness and littleness I saw on every hand. Thank God, he was working in my life to bring me to a spiritual breakthrough instead. In those months I read much about the Spirit-filled life. In February of 1970, I attended a conference where Dr.

Stephen Olford preached. There came the conviction that I should go to New York, spend some time with Dr. Olford, and seek this breakthrough to the Spirit-filled life. Dr. Olford invited me to attend the Christian Life Conference in March of that year in Calvary Baptist Church.

"I became more open to the Lord's guidance and desirous of the Spirit-filled life. Between that night in early February and the first week of March there came the realization that the infilling I had desired had come . . . quietly, deeply, and most meaningfully. In studying, praying, reading, and conversing with others I have become convinced that this Spirit-filled life is not something that just a few are to experience, but that God's desire is that all his childen live Spirit-filled lives. Life has become deeply meaningful and adventuresome as day by day I see God working through areas of my life he had been unable to penetrate before.

"The Spirit-filled life is a constant conviction of his inflowing power as one yields to him. It is a manifestation of the fruit of the Spirit—love, joy, peace, and longsuffering."

Frank Stovall, Music Professor at Southwestern Baptist Theological Seminary, Fort Worth, Texas, describes his experience:

"*All things new*—would be an appropriate description of recent developments in my Christian life. I was saved at a very early age and was exposed to excellent training with early growth in grace. Soon, however, personal ambition began to conflict with my commitment to Christ, and ambition won out. I remained active in church, but my commitment was to a point and no further. I would not participate in revival meetings because I did not want to face the hours of conviction that I knew would come in the services over my sin. I did not want to make the kind of commitment I knew Christ would require.

"It is alarming how far from God a person can get even though he is in Christian work. Severe crises were permitted by the Lord but my faith was weakened instead of being strengthened. I felt too guilty over past refusals to pray for God's help.

"What finally brought me to my knees was another person's problem. A student came to me with a serious problem. He had decided to literally sell out to Satan and turn his back on Christ. In my spiritual condition I was unable to help. I was defeated at the very point where I desired victory—in being a minister to help others. I entered a season of prayer which was broken only by work demands. I prayed for faith to believe God's Word. I was brought under deep conviction of my sins. I was praying for my friend but was finding answers for myself as well.

"I poured out my sins in a torrent of confession. I saw sins that had been in my life unconfessed and thus unforgiven. When the confession and forgiveness was complete I felt that tremendous release of inexpressible joy I had never known before. Jesus had become Sovereign Lord. Everything was new! What used to be a source of constant frustration now became joyous victory.

"The secret of the Christian life is making every day his and allowing him to live his life through me. Praise God, I don't have to try. He doesn't want my efforts. He wants my submission. I am resting the whole case with Jesus and stand ready to do anything and go anywhere. One of my greatest joys is that of sharing with students the joys of the Spirit-directed life!"

Beverly Terrell, gifted musician from Dallas, Texas, found the key to victory in a very painful way. Listen to her story:

"In the spring of 1963 God revealed to me that I had not allowed him to be 'Number One God' in my life. The commandment, 'Thou shalt have no other gods before me,' took on a life-changing significance.

"The instrument God used to bring me to this realization was one of those 'gods'—my singing voice. He took away my voice, and I entered a period of spiritual emptiness. For the first time in my life I experienced utter despair and had no where to turn but to the Lord.

"One day as I was cleaning the house, the Holy Spirit lifted the veil from my eyes and gave me a simple spiritual insight . . . the ability to see myself as he saw me. I saw spiritual pride and hypocrisy with self in control of my life. I had actually dethroned God and enthroned self as ruler of my whole existence. I fell to my knees in despair, confessing sin for what seemed an eternity of time. It was a true 'spiritual housecleaning.'

"From that time my life has undergone some amazing changes. My tensions, my volatile temper (which I had always excused as 'artistic temperment'), and my hypercritical spirit drifted away. A great hunger for the Word of God came, and the knowledge of his presence was real in daily prayer and devotions. As Christ became real to me, neighbors came to know Christ as Savior through natural witnessing.

"I will not use the vehicle of sacred music to my own selfish advantages ever again. I am aware, and gratefully so, that as I sing there is a depth and power to my singing that I had never known before.

"Perhaps the greatest thrill of all was that of seeing my three sons move into a faith of their very own as they related to the Holy Spirit.

"Thanks be to God, that I'm just beginning to know what Paul meant in Galatians 2:20 when he said, 'I am crucified with Christ; nevertheless I LIVE!!!' "

Cecil McGee was formerly employed by the Sunday School Board in Nashville, Tennessee. He is now engaged in drama evangelism and spiritual life conferences across the country. God has wrought a mighty work in his life and I am glad that you have the privilege of reading his testimony:

"God did a wonderful thing in my life on the morning of March 1, 1967, and since that time life has been fantastic, exciting, and a day-by-day experience with Jesus. The only thing that could possibly make it better would be the privilege of retracing my steps through the years and sharing my discovery with those whose lives I touched as a youth director, minister of music, educational director, and consultant for the Sunday School board for fifteen years. But the past is impossible to reclaim—not even one second of those twenty-five years.

"For thirty-five years I was a Christian and had no idea of the riches that were mine in Christ Jesus. I knew nothing to do but to work hard for God, striving to please him with a good performance. It was a legalistic relationship rather than one built on Father-son love. Reading the Bible was legalistic. I did it as a religious leader so I could check it on my Training Union record in order to set a good example. There was no hunger for the Word of God and no desire to pray. I would go for weeks without praying at all. Life was filled with constant ups and downs. I always rededicated my life in every revival and felt soothed for a moment but it lasted only a brief time . . . a few days or weeks at the most. I would then return to the same old rut.

"There were sins in my life over which I had absolutely no control—lust, pride, jealousy, envy, self-centeredness, lack of love, the desire to impress others.

"Five years ago I came in contact with the book by

Ian Thomas, *The Saving Life of Christ*. A friend of mine sat down with me and read to me the entire second chapter which dealt with the exchanged life—not I, but Christ. At the end of that reading, I knew that the deep hunger of my heart which had been there always, the emptiness that I had known spiritually all of my life, could be satisfied only through the Holy Spirit. During those moments to follow, the Holy Spirit said to me, 'You're hungry and empty . . . why don't you let me fill you?' My pride kept me from admitting to anyone that I, a religious leader, had any need. I started studying God's Word and three months later I had an encounter with the Lord Jesus that changed everything. God showed me my sins and the blackness of them. It was like a movie that morning—I saw them all—every one of them. I wept over them and laid them out before the Lord and for the first time in my life had the joy of *knowing* that my sins were forgiven. I claimed 1 John 1:9 and praised the Lord for making me clean and pure.

"For the first time in thirty-five years I knew what it was like to be free from guilt. I praised the Lord, obeyed the command of Romans 12:1, handed over to him the control of my life, and asked the Holy Spirit to fill my life.

"These have been wonderful years . . . four of them. The ups and downs are gone. There is constant peace, joy, and victory. The besetting sins have been conquered through his Spirit. 'Greater is he that is in you, than he that is in the world' (1 John 4:4). It is a day by day reality, moment by moment. What a thrill to begin each day with a fresh commitment to the Lord Jesus, thanking him for *literally* living within my body and praising him for victory over lust, pride, and the other onslaughts that will be coming my way through the day. And what a joy to come to the end of the day praising him for his goodness, confessing every known sin, and going to sleep committing myself to him all over again.

"Yes, God did a wonderful thing for me on the morning of March 1, 1967 and I praise him for a *new life in Jesus!*"

I want to close this chapter with a most exciting testimony. I continue to be amazed at the arrangements of God in bringing these testimonies together. It is fitting that such a testimony as the following should climax this parade of spiritual victories.

There is little doubt that one of the greatest revivals of our generation took place in the small town of West Plains, Missouri, in 1966. So dramatic was the moving of God on that little town that the West Plains *Daily Quill* carried the news of the revival in banner-type headlines, declaring "GOD IS ALIVE!" The first line of the story read, "Jesus Christ has invaded West Plains!" God's power was unleashed on this southwest Missouri town and the whole populace was caught in its spell.

The pastor there was Jim Hylton. He tells how God dramatically brought about his "funeral" and then the "fulness":

"I became pastor to Dr. Jeanette Beall in West Plains and she shared with me almost daily many of the events that had taken place in the great Shantung revival in the northern province of China. Through her stories I began to understand what real revival was all about.

"There was another lady in the church that I considered quite eccentric. Her vitality and vibrancy were contagious · She was used mightily of God as the intercessor for West Plains.

"God was to use a young man, whose name was Jay Davis, in addition to Dr. Beall and this little lady. In Campus Crusade for Christ Jay had come into the fulness of the Spirit. As he shared his testimony with me, I felt uneasy.

"The lives of these three people seemed to constantly haunt me. While they had joy and love with the fruit of the Spirit, my life was typified by a lack in all these areas. Despite the fact that during those days I had everything a young minister would ever want, a quiet desperation settled over me. I had no power with God and none with men.

"At a retreat in which I had a part in planning, there came the last session when only the program personnel showed up. A friend suggested that we spend the whole morning in prayer. God seized me in that prayer meeting and suddenly a cry burst from my throat, 'Oh, God, I'm sick . . . sick of it all and sick of myself. God, what's wrong?' I went home greatly distressed.

"In a revival a few weeks later the power of God began to move mightily and people began to get saved everywhere. Christians confessed their sins and made things right with each other. During a visit that week with a man who was considering leaving the church because it was 'cold and indifferent,' I reacted to my pride and refuted his accusation. In the midst of the verbal battle, the evangelist stood to rebuke us both. His words sank into my heart like an arrow. I saw my sinfulness and my wickedness as I never had before. I saw that there indeed was no good thing in me. I poured out my sin and gave up myself to God as I lay prostrate on the floor.

"How long we prayed I do not know. I do know that when I stood to my feet I was stripped of everything— reputation, degree, title, church, ministry . . . everything! I reckoned on Romans 6:6 which commands us to look upon ourselves as dead to sin but alive to God through Christ. I DIED THAT DAY! The man in whose home we were visiting was a *funeral director*. I died in the home of a funeral director!

"How different everything was after that. I no longer needed to prove anything. Glasses I had worn as a part of my ministerial mask somehow had gotten chipped. God said, 'Take them off.' I did and have not worn them since.

"Life has not been the same and will never be. My home has been transformed as well as my entire life. God touched down and touched me too!"

These are only twelve thrilling testimonies of the work of the Spirit of God in lives today. There could just as easily have been ten times this many. God is on the move! He is up to something! He is moving wonderfully in individual lives and transforming mere men and women into dynamic forces of exciting magnitude.

I trust that your testimony of God's touch upon your life is throbbing within your heart right now as you have finished reading about these. Praise the Lord!

PART III
IN THE PATH OF HIS MOVING
AREA ONE: REVIVAL IN THE PERSONAL
LIFE

The Holy Spirit is the power of revival. There is no revival without the free moving of the Spirit of God. The Spirit first begins to move within the heart of the individual. As he finds liberty in individuals, he then can create the qualities which lead to real revival. It is natural, then, that the most immediate and obvious of changes occur in the personal life.

As I reported in a previous chapter, revival began to take place in my life several years ago. I had heard of revival and had prayed for revival, but I certainly had no background to equip me to recognize it when it came. I found again more of the implications of what Jesus meant when he said, "The wind bloweth where it listeth, and thou hearest the sound thereof, but canst not tell whence it cometh, and wither it goeth: so is every one that is born of the Spirit" (John 3:8). I knew that "Holy Wind" was blowing, but I knew little else. I am thrilled to share with you some of the more obvious results in my own life that took place in the path of His moving.

Jesus has become Somebody real. How can I explain this to you? Jesus was to me Someone precious. This had always been true since I was a little boy. I had never had any other feelings for him but love. I would read of his miracles in my little storybook and love him more because of what he did. I had asked him into my life as Savior many years before. But, can you believe it, Jesus had never been really somebody real to me? He was a great hero in a great Book, and I worshiped him and served him and sought in every way to please him. But he was not real like I knew he could be and wanted to be. Maybe it was my idea of what a thing had to be to be real that kept him from being real to me. Things were real. Church work was real. Problems were real. Ministerial ambitions were real. Statistics, the gauges I used to assure my success, were real. A thousand other things were real, and it must have been that these things crowded out the reality of Christ for years.

But one night Jesus became real to me and has remained

very real from that moment to this. I believe that the moment I began to count as nothing all those things that were so important before, the reality of Christ began to dawn on my troubled soul. Now, I must confess to you that Jesus is more real to me than this page which you are reading. He is more real than the church I so gratefully serve. He is more real than the problems that confront me. He is more real to me at this very moment than he has ever been before. When I saw the emptiness of the things in which I found superficial security and threw them down before him, he became the greatest reality in my life. I go to sleep with this glorious reality flooding my heart and wake up with the first conscious thought being of his presence. Jesus Christ has become a glorious and unceasing reality!

The Bible has become a new Book. This was one of the first and most noticeable miracles to happen. It was as if I had blinked my eyes and God had exchanged books before my presence. It was immediate! Whole passages took on new meaning. Stories had new implications. The unity of the entire Bible began to be exciting. Whereas in times previous I scanned the pages of the Bible for prospective sermon material, now sermons literally jumped out of the pages at me. Preaching began to be a joyous overflow instead of a struggle. I seemed unable to say the words fast enough as truth came piling in upon me. I suppose I was afraid that as time went on the experience might become dull and the Bible lose its excitement. Instead, it has become through the years increasingly thrilling.

Old Testament passages have caught fire with meaning. Opening the Bible at any point is like tapping into a mighty current of divine life.

I have discovered that God wants me to go to the

Bible to receive what he would say to me through it. Then, my preaching is simply the rehearsal of what he has said to me and thus, is simply a situation in which the congregation overhears me talking to myself. They, like me, are in need of the Truth and are blessed by it. The Bible has become wonderfully alive!

Prayer has become an adventure. Before Christ became real, prayer and Bible reading were means of stacking up points in the system of devotion. I didn't particularly enjoy them, but if they pleased God, I certainly wanted to do that. But now, all of a sudden, prayer became fellowship with the living Lord. It became a tryst with the Trinity. I found myself talking to every member of the godhead, praising God, the Father, the Son, and the Holy Spirit. I had never known how to praise before. Now, it became natural and *the* most vital part of my prayer life.

In times past, praying was a means of begging God out of certain things I wanted. It was *contingent* and pleading in nature. Now it had become *certain* as I claimed the *nowness* of God's answers. Verses on prayer came alive, such as Isaiah 65:24, "And it shall come to pass, that before they call, I will answer; and while they are yet speaking, I will hear." There is no contingency in that verse. There is positive certainty.

Prayer is no longer *pleading* but *thanking*. God has already given us all things. We are but to appropriate them through the adventure of prayer as we need them. I cannot think of a prayer that Jesus Christ himself is *not* the answer to. He is God's unceasing *YES* to our need. "Christ is all and in all" (Col. 3:11).

The Psalms have become an effective means of praying and songs in the hymnal have become aids to personal worship of the Savior.

My Jesus, I love thee,
  I know Thou art mine,
For Thee all the follies
  of sin I resign:
My gracious Redeemer,
  my Saviour art Thou;
If ever I loved Thee,
  my Jesus, 'tis now.

Prayer has become warfare with Satan within the position with Christ in the heavenlies. Prayer is a victory as I come to claim. "This is the victory that overcometh the world, even our faith" (1 John 5:4).

Witnessing has become an inevitable pleasure. The task of witnessing had been an uncomfortable chore. It was never natural but always forced. It seemed to be an obligation that when fulfilled brought a measure of relief. But as the Spirit moved to take control, witnessing became a joyous overflow. I accidentally find more people who need Jesus now than I could on purpose before. Witnessing used to be a means of alleviating guilt; now it is an exciting overflow. I had all the soul-winning courses one could take. I read all the books I could find on how to win souls. But the day I woke up to the fact that I had the Winner of Souls living inside my body waiting to be released by my submission, witnessing became a *pleasure.*

A few minutes after I had finished the paragraph above, I heard a knock at the door. I was writing in a motel room, and the man at the door was there to make an adjustment on one of the lamps. I engaged him in conversation about the Savior, and in a few minutes he was on his knees at the foot of the bed asking Jesus to come into his heart. Reuben went away a living testimony of the power of Christ to save.

Problems that had haunted me were solved in Christ. I want to deal in the next few paragraphs with three great problems which I believe confront everyone of us.

The first is *depression.* I was almost a manic-depressive. I would have moods of depression brought on by small matters. I would often wake up deeply depressed and defeated in spirit. I could hardly face the tasks of the day. A dark cloud seemed to hang over my mind. The future seemed bleak. Everything took on the "blahs." I could do nothing to rid myself of the "blues." It was worse just after a spiritual victory or just before a spiritual blessing. It was tiring and frustrating.

When the Spirit began to move in my heart, I remember talking with the Lord about my depression. I had awakened to the glorious fact that Jesus Christ, in all that he was, lived in my heart. That had been a gladdening fact. I remember praying, "Lord, when I awaken in the morning, let the first thought that crosses my mind be— JESUS IS ALIVE IN ME TODAY TO BE IN ME ALL THAT I NEED TO BE AND ALL THAT THE FATHER REQUIRES ME TO BE. Let me say to you, 'This is your body. You possess it and fill it and run around in it today in full control minding your own business through it.'" And this is exactly what happened! The worst time of the day (getting-up time) became the best part because it was the beginning of the first day of the remainder of my life.

The stimulations to depression and discouragement continue. The response to those is different. With all that has happened, it might be added that *Satan has become as real as Jesus.* The recognition that it is not God that has given us the spirit of depression will help us deal with it. God gives us a spirit "of power, and of love and of a sound mind" (2 Tim. 1:7). All other kinds of spirits come from Satan. Recognizing the *source* will encourage us to go to our *resource*. I have found nothing quite as helpful in the matter of depression as the *therapy of thanksgiving*. Listen to this magnificent Scripture: "In every thing give thanks: for this is the will of God in Christ Jesus concerning you" (1 Thess. 5:18). Do you want to do the will of God? Then, give thanks! There is a vital change which takes place when we practice the *therapy of thanksgiving*.

I was talking with a mother about her boy. The situation was absolutely impossible. Hearts had been broken; there was shame and continued heartache. In the midst of her tears I asked, "Ruth, have you ever thanked God in the midst of all this?" She looked shocked with a sort of "what-kind-of-idiot-do-you-think-I-am?" countenance. I repeated the question. The answer that finally came revealed that she hadn't. I quoted that verse in 1 Thessalonians. I shared with her that the primary will of God for us in any situation was thanksgiving. He generally would not reveal his will beyond that until we *obeyed*. We prayed, and for the first time she thanked God in the midst of this heartbreaking situation. There was immediate relief that this was a turning point in her life.

The second matter I want to discuss here is *distress*. Distress differs from depression in that it seizes one rather suddenly and causes reactions that have serious consequences. One may go from distress to depression or guilt. It usually happens in this manner:

You are doing fine and everything is going fine. Then tragedy strikes. Unwelcomed events come crashing in upon your life. Someone says something. A bit of bad news comes. A number of things pile up. It is here that the *therapy of thanksgiving* works again.

Allow another personal reference. In 1967 we received as a gift a new automobile. In August of that year we began a long-awaited vacation to California. Everything was fine with the new car, and ample funds for an unforgettable vacation were ours. About 120 miles out of San Antonio at about 2:00 A.M., a big West Texas deer darted out in front of us. The collison was unavoidable. The point of impact was right between the headlights. The hood flew up . . . the air conditioner blew up and with it, I supposed, our vacation! I had learned that verse, "In every thing give thanks . . ." a few weeks before. To me it was just another Scripture passage until that morning. I was plainly in *distress*. Had I done the normal, natural thing I would have gone back, seized the poor dead deer, and slapped him a time or two; I would have then proceeded to get angry at everybody in the car just on general principles; and then, I would have continued to make life miserable for myself and all those about me. But would you believe what happened? God brought that passage to my consciousness as quick as a flash of lightning. "This is God's will," I said, "I want to do God's will!" Right then and there I thanked God in the midst of that awful situation. Now, remember, you don't have to see anything to be grateful *for* in order to be thankful *in* a situation. If you will be thankful *in* circumstances, God will soon show you something to be grateful *for*. Immediately (or sooner) upon obedience to God's will, there fell upon the whole situation a mantle of peace and joy such as I had not known before. We had a blast! We laughed and played and joked and prayed. In less than twelve hours we were on our way in another car with everything cared for!

When distress comes, many people try to conceive what Christ would do in the situation. They then try to do what they think he would do. This is a farce because this Christ is alive in us at that very moment of distress. Why not find out what he would do by *letting him do it?* Don't react; let him! My Lord, living in me and filling my life with himself, settles the problems of distress.

The third matter for our consideration is *deficiency.* How many people are haunted by feelings of deficiency. "I feel so inadequate!" is the hopeless cry of thousands. Satan would have us respond to this feeling of inadequacy with defeat and resignation. I learned one day this shocking lesson: I *SHOULD* FEEL INADEQUATE IF I *AM* INADEQUATE . . . AND I AM! So why live in the *feeling?* Why not just face the *fact?* Our sin is not in feeling inadequate but in expecting ourselves to be adequate. God certainly doesn't expect us to be adequate! For this reason he provided the indwelling Christ and the fulness of the Holy Spirit to make adequacy in him possible.

I am then to accept the fact of my inadequacy and praise the Lord for *his* adequacy in me. What a wonderful arrangement that he has provided for all of us. Our deficiency is the grounds on which his *sufficiency* can be demonstrated. God's power shows up best in weak people. Our *ignorance* is the stage on which his *wisdom* can be manifested. Jesus Christ is God's great *positive* to all our *negatives.* This realization is what moved Paul to say, "Most gladly therefore will I rather glory in my infirmities, that the power of Christ may rest upon me" (2 Cor. 12:9). With the moving of the Spirit, our deficiencies are cared for.

To be noticed, also, in the path of the Spirit's moving is *reality of the fruit of the Spirit.* The fruit of the Spirit cannot be fabricated. The Living Letters translation puts it like this, "But when the Holy Spirit controls our lives he will produce this kind of fruit in us: love, joy, peace, patience, kindness, goodness, faithfulness, gentleness, and self control" (Gal. 5:22). In John 7:37-39, Jesus promised that as we drank of him and believed, out of us would flow rivers of living water. He was speaking of the Spirit which we would receive. Therefore, we can gladly sing:

> I've got LOVE *like a river* in my soul . . .
> I've got JOY *like a river* in my soul . . .
> I've got PEACE *like a river* in my soul . . .

In the path of his moving, this blessed cluster of fruit will inevitably grow!

It has been my privilege to observe phenomenal transformations in the lives of people within the fellowship. I believe that it would be helpful to the reader to hear some of these vital witnesses of revival in the personal life.

James Ennis, associate pastor, Castle Hills Baptist Church, reports:

"Sick and tired of being sick and tired (familiar words!) . . . that was myself up until December, 1969. My feelings and attitudes went up and down with the attendance, offerings, and additions to the church. It was drive, drive, drive, and push, push, push. I felt surely that the Lord had more for me!

"When Bertha Smith came to speak of the filling with the Spirit, I realized that I had been going in my own strength most of the time. It was myself and not the Spirit's power. That was the reason my life was full of ups and downs.

"The Spirit revealed sins that I had to confess. I also confessed that I had been on the throne of my life most of the time and told the Lord that I was quitting. I wanted him to fill my life from head to toe. When I gave up to him, he did just that! Praise the Lord, it hasn't been the same since that night in December!"

Malcolm Grainger, minister of music, Castle Hills Baptist Church, testifies:

"My first week on the field at Castle Hills happened to be Week of Prayer for Foreign Missions. Bertha Smith was to be the speaker. It was under her ministry that the Holy Spirit began his completing work on me.

"When we were asked to list our sins, I was reluctant. I prepared my list very objectively until we were given a little tract, "Not I, But Christ." After reading this tract my sin list became very subjective. In fact, I saw myself for the first time as Paul saw himself, 'for I know that in me (that is, in my flesh) dwelleth *no* good thing.' The Holy Spirit revealed that I was like an unclean cup and all the 'good' I ever attempted to do for God was contaminated by what *I* was. Only what Christ does is acceptable to the Father. I was led to claim three things: (1) To reckon myself dead and thank him for having accomplished it; (2) I asked him to sit on the throne of my heart; and (3) I asked him to fill me with his Holy Spirit. I claimed it and thanked him for it. There was then and is now a sweet rest, walking in the fulness of his Spirit. I would not change one moment of his control for all the yesterdays which were wasted and barren."

Ann Rollwitz, youth director, Castle Hills Baptist Church, witnesses:

"There was no continuing joy in my life. I was up when things were well but defeated and depressed when problems and trials presented themselves. It was through Trumbull's book, *Victory in Christ,* that I saw myself as I was. The whole of my life was activity for activity's sake. I knew that I had been saved by doing absolutely nothing but by an act of my will asking Jesus to do what he said he would do and claiming that he had done exactly that. When I received him into my heart, I had received all there was and that included the Holy Spirit.

"Thus I saw that all I needed to live out the Christian life was to ask God for the filling of the Spirit, and since he already wanted me to be filled, I had only to thank him for it. I confessed my sins (a long list), acknowledged Christ as Lord, choosing death to self. I asked to be filled and thanked him for doing just what he said. What a revelation!

"Has it made a difference? As much as night and day! The joy, peace, and love are in abundance just exactly as he said it would be. This is only the beginning. God is continually taking me through the growth processes to make me broken bread and poured out wine. Praise the Lord!"

It is a joy beyond measure to work with these and other staff members who are allowing Christ to control their lives. I can testify to the greatness of the work of Christ in the lives of these! It is glorious!

Mildred Mills, pastor's secretary, Castle Hills Baptist Church, testifies:

"Willing to 'do my very best,' as I stated in the interview, I began my work as pastor's secretary. That 'trying to do my best' continued until December of 1969 when I prayed with Bertha Smith. I confessed my sins and, most of all, the sin of 'doing my best.' I became free and cleansed and asked him to fill me with his Holy Spirit, and he did. I stopped trying and started trusting, which is nothing but victory!"

The man I would have nominated least likely to get caught up in the revival was *Eugene Burrows,* now chair-

man of the deacons at Castle Hills Baptist Church. Gene
was the picture of human confidence and sufficiency. But
God has wrought a mighty work in him! Listen to his
testimony:

"The words of the hymn refer to me . . . 'Years I
spent in vanity and pride' . . . and they include the years
after I was saved. Now I see in them conditions as they
really were: honest efforts, but wholly mine, and though
they sprang from a desire to serve God and to be the
right kind of father and husband, they were doomed from
the start.

"My own thoughts, my own ambitions, my own concept of what was proper and improper; saved but filled
with self; redeemed but rebelling against his lordship . . .
from these filthy rags I blindly sought success. But, praise
his name, he still loved me and desired for me the very
best . . . his Spirit filling, fulfilling, and directing me.

"God used something I loved to bring about my yielding to him. A serious heart defect in one of my twenty-
two-year-old twin daughters, followed by heart surgery,
almost resulted in her death. Man's efforts were inadequate. My continued prayer caused me to see the desperate need in my own life. When all hope appeared to be
gone, faith, that fruit of the Spirit, made it possible for
me to claim recovery on the basis of Mark 11:24, and
in thirty-six hours recovery followed.

"Some months later his Spirit brought about that victory which is total and complete when based on surrender
to him, when on my knees with my pastor I asked that
the Holy Spirit fill my life and take control.

"What peace comes when I no longer have to depend
on my own efforts to do his will; what confidence there
is in each day because the Lord is in control, doing his
will in my life, bringing, as he promised, the 'abundant

life' (John 10:10). Praise his Name!' "

The life of Gene Burrows is one of the great miracles of this revival!

Another deacon in our church tells this experience:

"I had been confronted with the matter of the Spirit-filled life before. But during the time when I was studying to be ordained as a deacon in our church, I realized that though I had Christ in my heart, I had never let him have complete control of my life. For the first time I understood that for Christ to have full control of my life, I must die to my self-will. There was resistance, and the devil used every resource available to keep me from surrendering. But, for once, I sincerely desired God's will to be done more than any time I could recall. I confessed to God that I had been the lord of my life, and I confessed sins, present and past, in my life. I asked him to forgive me and take control of my life.

"I can say without a doubt that on that night Christ did take control of my life. I could not begin to explain the change that has taken place in my life since that night. The next day this same experience came to my wife. We have never known such joy and happiness as now with Jesus as Lord of our lives. He has totally revolutionized our lives! Praise the Lord!"

A schoolteacher witnesses:

"In April of 1970 a great change came over our church and myself. The Holy Spirit convicted me of hatred for someone in our church. Someone read the verse which says, 'If a man say I love God and hateth his brother, he is a liar.' I knew that I had to get right and made the apology necessary. In a prayer meeting after that I learned what it was to 'die to self.' Christ was then free to fill me and to live through me.

"The big change was in the realm of witnessing. I had

not been bold. When I was filled with the Spirit, the Lord was able to do things through me that I had been unable to do in my own strength."

A housewife, now a powerful witness for Christ, reports a transforming work in her life:

"I wondered how I could serve Jesus. I began to understand that though I had Jesus living in my heart, I was not letting him have control of my life. In fact, there were a few things I loved more than Jesus. But one day I knelt to give up to Christ and asked him to do with me what he desired. He gave me a hunger and thirst for his Word and a consuming desire to see souls saved. I thank God for saving me, filling me, and using me."

Praise the Lord for co-workers who have found the secret! Secretaries, custodians, deacons, members, and everybody testify to the "joy unspeakable and full of glory."

Mrs. Helen Cade, our Spirit-filled church visitor, leads people to Christ almost every day. As the Holy Spirit has moved in our midst, few days have gone by without people being saved somewhere within the outreach ministry of the church. We will speak of the church later.

PART III
IN THE PATH OF HIS MOVING
AREA TWO: REVIVAL IN THE HOME

The home has been the location of the greatest miracle in the whole revival! Had you asked me several months ago if I had a happy home, I would have replied in the affirmative with enthusiasm. What I did not know at the time was that when the Spirit of God comes to take over a home, there is a measure of joy present that we had no occasion to know before.

The glorious visitation of the Lord really began in April of 1970 in our church as we shall later discuss. I had always considered that when revival came, everything else would automatically slide into its proper position all by itself. The home and all its relationships would surely fit into this category. Well, it didn't! In fact, revival brought a new level of excitement and business that took me out of the home more and more. Barbara (my wife) began to find increasing resentment inevitable. I resented her resentment. We both had experienced a new level of commitment in our lives but did not seem to be able to apply this commitment to the running of the household and in our personal relationships. We seemed to have victory everywhere but at home and with each other.

As the revival progressed, the situation at home regressed! As we struggled to find the solution, little did we know that we were on the edge of the greatest discovery of the seventeen years of our married lives. The crisis seems always to precede the victory. Our crisis came one Friday evening with a misunderstanding that deepened into mutual despair. We were unable to communicate. On our way home from a social function we went by the church and knelt at the kneeling rail to pray together. Our prayers seemed alike, incapable of getting through, but I remember praying one prayer, "Lord, we claim a miracle for our home." We left the church for home with little relief in our despair.

After taking the baby-sitter home, we continued our discussion. Finally Barbara opened the Bible to Ephesians 5 and remarked, "Jack, is this what is wrong? Have I just not submitted to you?" I replied that I didn't think

she had. We had been through this a good while before
and thought that it was settled.

All of a sudden it seemed that with the opening of
the Bible, God took over the discussion. We began to
read the verses before and after verse 22 which says,
"Wives, submit yourselves unto your own husbands, as
unto the Lord." Our eyes began to open. We had never
dealt with the verse in context. We went back to verse
18 which says, "And be not drunk with wine, wherein
is excess; but be filled with the Spirit." When we began
to follow the sequence of truths presented in line with
this command, we discovered to our delight the order
of victory for the home. We discovered that being filled
with the Spirit is a matter of *taking a step* as well as
walking. Follow me as we take the steps to victory in
the home:

THE FULNESS OF THE SPIRIT

We have discussed this already, but we cannot repeat
it too often. The fulness of the Spirit is the order of the
day for every believer. Thus, in the home the husband
must be filled with the Spirit and the wife must be filled
with the Spirit. This is the first step in the order of victory.
It is delightful to know also that children can come to
realize the meaning of the Spirit's control over their lives.
But just to say that everyone in the home has been filled
with the Spirit is not to assume that there will be instant
victory without other meaningful steps being taken.

HARMONIOUS COMMUNICATION AND
CONSTANT THANKSGIVING

After the experience of fulness, Paul indicates that there
will be communication of the highest order. He says,
"Speaking to yourselves in psalms and hymns and spirit-

ual songs, singing and making melody in your heart to the Lord" (Eph. 5:19). The Spirit brings communication. This communication is between all people, between us and the Lord, and between husband and wife. The trouble with most marriages is the breakdown of communication. Problems are not the problem in marriage. It is the inability to communicate regarding the problem that makes the problem. Our marriage was no exception.

THE MIRACLE OF MUTUAL SUBMISSION

"Submitting yourselves one to another in the fear of God" (v.21). It hit us like the proverbial "ton of bricks." We had assumed this but had never experienced it. Barbara took a look at me and said, "I think I could submit to you, but you have a lousy (exact word) record." I replied, "Your record is not so hot itself." (This conversation was firm but kind.) Then we looked at the verse again and were hit between the eyes with the last six words, "IN THE FEAR OF THE LORD."

We were to submit to each other on the basis of our fear of God, not on each other's "lousy" record. We immediately came into possession of a new kind of fear of the Lord. We looked at each other and thought, Though I cannot submit to you because of you, I can submit to you because of him. We had been waiting for a reason in each other to mutually submit and it had not come.

We discovered that if Christ is in the husband and in control, it is Christ who does the submitting. If Christ is in the wife and in control, it is Christ within the wife to whom the Christ in the husband submits. Now, turning these facts around will mean that the wife will find Christ within her submitting to the Christ in the husband.

This may sound like double talk, but it leads to "double thrill" within the home. Don't pass over it lightly. Barbara and I began to feel an intense desire to allow Christ within us such freedom that he could bring about this miracle of mutual submission. We came to acknowledge that it takes two to consent for this miracle to come to pass. "Submitting yourselves one to another" more than implies mutual consent and mutual volition. Realizing that we had never really done this in the seventeen years of our married lives, we decided that this was the time. We got on our knees together and looked into each other's eyes. I said to her, "Barbara, I submit myself wholly to you." She followed suit, doing the same thing. We then came to the shocking relization that in spiritual mathematics . . . ONE PLUS ONE EQUALS ONE!

We had read how it was God's will that "they two should be one flesh," but in the process of trying to be one, we had trouble deciding which one! In truth, the answer is neither one! And only when the Christ within one as Lord submits himself to Christ in the other as Lord is there one . . . *and that one is CHRIST!* Neither husband nor wife survives the collision with Christ. He is the only one left. It is like the melting together of two pieces of metal with the heat of submission being occasion and means of the unity. This submission involves the totality of the life.

Then, we are ready for the next step.

WIVES, SUBMIT

How repulsive that looks to the average wife! Looking at her husband, she is likely to ask, "Do you expect me to completely submit to that?" That command must be taken in context with the previous verse (v. 21). *Mutual* submission is the foundation for *wifely* submission. As two have submitted their lives to each other, there is then freedom to follow the plan of God for maximum joy in the home. Again there is a key phrase, namely, "as unto the Lord." If Christ is in the husband, it is as "unto the Lord" that the wife is submitting. If that husband is filled with the Spirit, then he has been dominated by divine life and for him to live is for Christ to live. For him to be husband is for Christ, in reality, to be the husband.

Wives who have husbands who are not saved report that they have a grave problem here. They must remember that in the divine order of things the submission of the wife is an absolute command. If the husband is not a Christian, the wife can still submit "as unto the Lord," her submission being a symbol of her relationship with Christ. This will be the clearest testimony of her relationship to Christ. If that husband is going to be won, the testimony of a submissive wife is evidence he needs to help him decide!

My wife is admittedly a person with a strong will. She does not easily submit. But when we saw the truth together and constructed the foundation with mutual submission, she submitted to her husband totally for the very first time in her life. There were no bright lights and music. There wasn't even a sensation of a rush of sentiment. But something very vital to the happiness of a home happened. A wife took her place, allowing her husband to take his! She crowned him king (in Christ) of the home. Man is incomplete without the woman and is made complete by her. Woman is incomplete without the man and is completed by him. Mutual submission brings two beings made for each other into one being, each joining the other to become a complete whole. The submission of the wife frees the husband to become the head of which she is the body. She finds that every king needs a queen, and she is his immediate choice! What she might have sought for in a thousand ways and never found, she finds in the act of crowning the husband as head of the home. The whole chemistry of the marriage is balanced and healthy.

HUSBANDS, LOVE!

The steps follow in order so that the submission of each to the other frees the wife to be submissive to the husband. Then the submission of the wife clears the way for the husband to love as he has never loved before. He is to love his wife as Christ loved the church and gave himself for it. He is made complete by her submission, and she is made complete by his love. He becomes the man he was made to be. She becomes the woman she was made to be. It is impossible to have victory in a marriage without the fulness of the Spirit, the spiritual communication which results, the mutual submission which follows, and the submission-love relationship which is allowed.

We joyfully discovered that when our relationship was full, the relationships with the children were transformed. Children can be filled with the Spirit and can grow with a deepening sensitivity to what it means to have Jesus Christ in control of the life. In coming to his fulness, they become veritable treasures of wisdom for parents. Nobody is an authority on the viewpoints of children like Spirit-filled children. We are busily becoming experts on children without their wisdom. Nobody in the world can help us help children like children who have discovered the key to triumphant living.

My children at this writing are aware that the Spirit can control a life. They have found the key! It fits every lock in their lives as well.

We have had a miracle in our home. It is more than a theory or a plan. It really works!

PART III
IN THE PATH OF HIS MOVING
AREA THREE: REVIVAL IN THE CHURCH

When the Holy Spirit moves in the church, it is like mutiny in reverse. I had been praying for revival for a long time. Revival is to the corporate body of Christ what the fulness of the Spirit is to the individual body of Christ, the believer.

This is the story of revival in a church, not a series of meetings but REVIVAL. The last chapter cannot be written because it has not yet happened. We pray that the revival will continue until Jesus comes. We will observe three facets of the revival: (1) The Road to Revival, (2) The Realities in Revival, and (3) The Results of Revival.

THE ROAD TO REVIVAL

Meet the Castle Hills Baptist Church. She is a teenager, sixteen years old—an unpredictable, awkward, impossible teen-ager. But she's really no different from most other teen-agers except that something vital has happened in her life.

I have been her pastor for all but two and one-half of her sixteen years. I would like to tell you about that experience of revival in her life.

The road to revival, wherever you begin, is the same. It begins with a burden. It may be on the part of one or many, but there is always a *burden*. This burden develops over the disparity between things as they are and things as they should be. We have no trouble assessing things as they are, but sometimes we find difficulty in agreeing on things as they should be. The dynamic, depth,

and direction of the church of the book of Acts should
be a fair start for things as they should be. There is no
reason that we in the twentieth century should comforta-
bly tolerate a declining church when the same Holy Spirit
who empowered the church of Acts waits to dwell in
and control the body, the church of today.

A few years ago we had a little rash break out on
the skin of civilization in the "God-is-dead" philosophy.
I suppose this was when my burden reached its peak
for revival. I really didn't blame the theologians for the
philosophy. It seemed almost inevitable. I just figured
that these self-appointed coroners of Christendom had
done their work and made a pronouncement from the
best of their limited recognition. They had examined the
body of God (the church) and had simply found no vital
signs of life. The announcement was unavoidable. "GOD
IS DEAD!"

"God, I know you are not dead. I still feel a pulse in
your body. Show them that you are alive and well!" was
my deep prayer. There had been revival in my heart,
and I was sensing that a new spirit of concern was beginning to generate. The God-is-dead announcement seemed
to mark the spot where the ebb of Christianity ran its
lowest in our century. It seemed that the tide had gone
all the way out. That tide was going to come back in!

Lord, do it again! Do it again! There was no reason
why he shouldn't and no reason why he couldn't. Therefore, I concluded that He *should* and *could* and *would!*
There were signs of a deep stirring among the people
of God. There was an increasing burden among the inter-
cessors. There also began to be *brokenness.* If God would
sow the seed of revival, the ground must be broken. The
burden became desperate. This brokenness came to its
deepest level in 1969 when the Holy Spirit and Bertha

Smith visited our church. A few of God's people entered into the agonies of Gethsemane's death. It was during that week I honored the Holy Spirit in praise for the first time for filling my life (though the experience had actually occurred several years before). The whole staff of the church was mightily dealt with by the Lord.

In February of 1970 we held a staff prayer retreat. We briefly laid plans for the year and then made a study of the little book entitled, *The Threefold Secret of the Holy Spirit,* and went to prayer. The Spirit of intercession seized us and laid us out in weeping. It was there that God confirmed that revival was indeed on the way.

For the next days there was a spirit of expectancy. On Easter Sunday, 1970, a crusade with Bob Harrington began in our church. At the Easter sunrise service, Evelyn Linton was in attendance. Her palatial mansion looked out upon the GPM Plaza where the service was being held. She had seen the lights and seemed drawn to the meeting. It was a cold Easter morning, and the service was necessarily brief. Bob preached less than five minutes and then led the large crowd in the sinner's prayer. Evelyn prayed this prayer and was mightily moved. Evelyn and her husband, Guy Linton, were the proprietors of the largest striptease night-club in town. The Green Gate club. Bob Harrington had preached in their club on a previous visit to San Antonio two years before. This time they invited him to preach at the club again. In the meanwhile they invited him to be a guest in their home for the week.

Because of crowded conditions the revival was moved from the church to a nearby athletic center where many people were saved. On Saturday afternoon, after a video-taped debate between Bob Harrington and noted atheist Madelyn Murray O'Hair, we returned to the Linton

home. Mrs. Linton was our guest as we watched and
listened to the debate. She had remarked after the debate,
"After watching and listening to Mrs. O'Hair, I know
I want to be a Christian." In the Linton home at 3:15
P.M. on April 4, 1970, Guy and Evelyn Linton, Bob Harrington, my wife, and I knelt at the coffee table where
Guy and Evelyn gave their lives to Jesus Christ. That
night they attended the services and made their professions of faith openly. There was cheering and weeping
as the announcement was made that The Green Gate
proprietors had received Christ as their Savior and that
The Green Gate would be closed immediately. The news
of their conversion and of the closing of the club caught
the city in shock! The Master of Ceremonies of the club,
Tom Zarzour, was saved at the closing ceremonies. (His
stage name was Danny Bishop.) The Lintons, Tom, and
many others made their professions at the church the
next morning and presented themselves for membership.
The meeting was extended another evening with more
people saved.

It was the following Sunday, April 12, when the fire
fell upon the church. I had preached a revival on the
campus of Texas A. & M. University the week previous
to that Sunday. I had heard the testimony of David Perry
about the revival that broke out on the campus of Asbury
College in Wilmore, Kentucky. I came back to preach
on April 12 with the conviction that God was ready to
do it again! God was up to something! We wanted to
be in on what he was up to! From the first service at
8:15 A.M. until the close of the final service of the day,
which ended at far past 10:00 P.M., there was a spiritual
visitation unlike anything we had ever experienced before.
There was open confession of sin with folks apologizing
to each other all over the place. The youth service was

supposed to end at 10:30 for youth Sunday School, but there was no stopping the Spirit of God. The youth simply moved out on the lawn in front of the church to continue the service of confession and praise. The final morning service saw the same thing happen. Hundreds of people were on their knees praying and confessing. Without a doubt, something had happened.

On Sunday evening, Tom Zarzour was to sing his first religious song! He had a beautiful voice but did not know one Christian song. Brother Malcolm Grainger, our music director, taught him "Jesus Loves Me." He sang it that night, and as he sang tears blurred his vision, and he lost sight of the words. He made up his own, and by the time he was through almost everybody was in tears. My associate, Brother James Ennis, was to have preached. He didn't preach. I asked him later what he did. He replied, "I just yelled REPENT four times and got out of the way." The service lasted for over three hours. THAT WAS THE BEGINNING OF A NEW ERA FOR OUR CHURCH.

THE REALITIES OF REVIVAL

Several words characterize revival wherever it breaks out. *Confession* seems always to be both a means and a part of genuine revival. Little sins could no longer be tolerated and were confessed and forsaken. Broken fellowship between people had to be repaired. The presence of the Spirit of God seemed to make hearts super sensitive to the slightest sin that had not been confessed and forgiven.

Testimony broke out in the midst of worship services and continues as folks who were reticent before boldly declare a newfound relationship with Jesus. As testimonies are given, not only in the church but in other places out across the country, God seems to use the word of revival to spark the desire everywhere. Sent out since the revival began, teams have been to churches across Texas and to some places out of the state.

Praise became a reality in worship. *Spontaneity* seemed to be in order as the Spirit continued his visitation. There was *liberty* and continuing *expectancy* in the services. There was a new *joy* to be noticed among the Christians. The singing took on a new vitality as we sang such songs as "Sweeping This Way" and "There's a Sweet, Sweet Spirit in This Place."

THE RESULTS OF REVIVAL

Many of the occasions of revival remain as the results of revival. I would summarize the results of revival in three statements:

There is a NEW DYNAMIC. That dynamic is the power of the Holy Spirit. Things happen every week that cannot be explained by human ability or human persuasion. There is an atmosphere of his presence that many have noticed as they have driven on the parking lot for the first time. This is not by human design. God is here and things occur which can be explained in no other terms than his presence.

Under this new dynamic we have seen things happen without being planned, programed, or promoted. From the day the revival broke out, there has not been one Sunday without people being saved and hardly a day in which there has not come word of someone being saved. There is a new dynamic in personal witnessing as well as prayer. A new and deepening sensitivity is developing of the work of Satan in seeking to thwart revival. Many have declared, and I agree, that the Spirit has done more in these months of revival than in all the years of the church's history combined.

We have seen alcoholics instantaneously delivered and become committed Christians and faithful church members. We have seen Buddhists come to Christ and go out to their homeland in Vietnam to become his missionaries. We have witnessed former Satan worshipers come to Jesus and become devout soldiers of the cross.

Young people by the score have come to Christ and boldly witness for him wherever they go. The Jesus Movement is not without beginnings in San Antonio.

Since revival began in april of 1970, another striptease club owner and his wife have been saved. Tommy Thomas was saved on Saturday night, June 20, and closed his club the same night. His wife, who had danced as the featured stripper, got right with God and has become a soul-winner.

Over fifteen show business personalities have been saved, several of them former strippers. They have become vital and joy-filled Christians. A carnival owner gave his heart to Christ recently and cleaned up his carnival to find that his first few weeks as a Christian carnival owner were the best in the history of the business.

One of the worst alcoholics in San Antonio was led down the aisle by two friends after prayer meeting one evening and found Christ as Savior immediately. He is a vital and vocal Christian and consistently faithful to his church.

In a three month period, a little band of women from the church, visiting in the county hospital, led over eighty people to faith in Christ.

A few months ago a hard-core hippie district opened to the witness of the gospel. Since that time over sixty of these young people have trusted Christ and many have been baptized into the membership of our church. A ministry to troubled teens has developed on the Tommy Thomas ranch as these young people are rehabilitated from drugs to responsible Christian living.

In a recent program to raise money for building projects, a primary goal of $300,000 was set to be raised over a period of three years. A challenge goal was set at $350,000. Both goals were surpassed, and another goal entitled the "hallelujah goal" was set at $400,000, which was promptly met. The final goal was a "Jesus is Lord" goal set at $500,000, which was also met and passed. With revival land the Spirit's visitation there is a *new dynamic.*

Secondly, there is a NEW DEPTH. With the coming of the Spirit of power, there is the sense of urgency about spiritual things. There is a new depth of hunger for the Word of God. On Thursdays a large number of ladies (and some men) meet for a one-hour study called "Dimensions in Christian Living," a study of the Spirit-filled life. On Sunday evenings there is a study entitled "Dealing with the Devil."

There is a new depth of prayer. Prayer meeting attendance has greatly increased. Prayer groups meet almost every day of the week. Young people have begun prayer meetings in some of the high schools. On Saturday evenings the young people gather at the church to pray. There has not been a prayer meeting yet without someone being saved. A special intercessory prayer chain is activated at a moment's notice, and over a hundred people are notified within minutes of a prayer need. Every moment of work on this book has been wrapped in prayer by a special intercessory prayer group.

There is a new depth of spiritual warfare and opposition, and, with this, there is a new confidence in the power of the Lord.

Thirdly, there is a NEW DIRECTION. When God knocks the statistical props from under us, there is in exchange a new set of motivations and goals. Involvement in all types of outreach ministries seems inevitable under the Spirit's leadership. The church, already involved in Latin American missions, in drug addict ministries among the hard core addicts as well as young people, and in ministries to orphaned children, is destined to become involved in more areas than these.

The ministry of a church in revival cannot be confined to its locale. Visitors almost every Sunday come to "see what's going on."

There is so much more that could be said. You ask, "What is the key?" The answer is, "The Spirit of God has begun to raise the body of Christ to normal life. The key is Christ in you . . . Christ in me . . . the hope of glory! Revival can happen anywhere there are those who desire it more than anything else in life. The promise is secure. God is waiting to bless his people. A mighty revial is sweeping this way!"

PART III
WORDS OF WARNING IN SEASONS OF BLESSING

This is a word of warning. No season is more flanked with perils than the season of great spiritual blessing. This is the time that Satan hates the most and is most eager to catch the believer off guard. If Satan cannot hold him back, he will push him to extremes and confu-

sion. Satan is highly dissatisfied with revival conditions
and will mobilize every kind of opposition against that
person or church in such a season of blessing.

This is not a word of pessimism. There is no room
for such in the Christian faith. It is a caution against
carelessness, a little of which can cost the Kingdom much.

I could trust that this chapter be used as a reference
in seasons of blessing. I could have hoped for such a
word of warning as revival came to our church. Surely
I could have missed some of these perils! We will simply
observe the nature of these problems and discuss them
briefly.

IGNORANCE OF SATAN'S DEVICES

If Satan has never been detected as a real and personal
adversary, revival will cause him to show himself. The
one continuous weakness of Satan is that he overdoes
it. He overdid it at Calvary. Believing that he had gotten
victory, he pressed the death of Jesus. But had he known
everything, he would not have crucified the Lord of glory.
The ignorance of Satan's devices as well as Satan, himself,
is appalling among believers of today. In case after case
where revival has broken out, one of Satan's favorite devices, employed and undetected, has been used to stop
it. He is a hinderer, a deceiver, and an accuser. Peter
declares that he walks about like a lion, seeking whom
he may devour (1 Pet. 5:8). Paul discusses the spiritual
warfare and warns us to stand strong with the full armour
of the Christian (Eph. 6:10-17).

There are many people who are not even certain that
there is an adversary, much less a war! Satan doesn't
bother folks like these. Why should he? They are not
bothering him!

I heard a friend say that if you got up and did not

meet the devil this morning it was a sure sign that you both were headed in the same direction! Now there is a shocking thought!

We have found it an absolute necessity to enter into an in-depth study of Satan. There has been no study more instantaneously beneficial and heartily responded to than our study of Satan. Hundreds of people have discovered a new level of victory through a knowledge of the authority of the believer over the devil. People, who have been intimidated for years, have learned to exercise their rights of position in Christ and dislodge the devil from places he has held for years!

When the disciples came back from their first mission, they exclaimed, "Lord, even the devils are subject unto us through thy name" (Luke 10:17). The Master seemed to respond without excitement, "I beheld Satan as lightning fall from heaven. Behold, I give unto you power to tread on serpents and scorpions, and over all the power of the enemy: and nothing shall by any means hurt you" (Luke 10:18-19). That last word is a marvelous promise which most folks act as if they don't believe. Think of it! The devil cannot hurt us! But watch out, because, if we are ignorant of his devices, he can cause us to hurt ourselves.

There are two common mistakes regarding the devil. The one is to *overrate* him. The other is equally dangerous—to *underrate* him. The secret of meeting and defeating Satan is simply the grant secret of the Christian faith—CHRIST IN YOU, THE HOPE OF GLORY!

SPIRITUAL PRIDE

I have heard it said that there are at least four kinds of pride. There is *face* pride, *race* pride, *place* pride, and *GRACE* pride. If pride can be so categorized, doubtlessly the most subtle is grace pride. It is that puffed-up pleasure with spiritual superiority. Do you realize that this is the one area where there can be no experts? The moment one becomes an expert in his own eyes, spiritually he is disqualified by pride.

In seasons of intense spiritual blessing, it is quite simple to get caught up in the sheer pride of being blessed and to look upon others with a sort of pitying sorrow.

Many times the believer who has discovered the key to triumphant living speaks a word of criticism about the one who has not made the discovery. We could easily assume that the reason the Lord seems to be blessing us more than some others is that we are more "blessable" than they. The truth is that we are no better than the most carnal of Christians.

The only cure to pride is true humility. True humility is not self-effacement or self-loathing. It is simply living with the fact that we are nothing and can do nothing; that Christ is doing it all and shall have all the glory to himself. The life of victory and conditions of revival owe all their reason for existing to him and him alone. No one on the face of the earth can take the least of the credit. This is the Lord's doing, and it is marvelous to our eyes!

Many a spiritual victory has been lost through a moment of pride and a lack of caution about it. "Wherefore let him that thinketh he standeth take heed lest he fall" (1 Cor. 10-12).

ENAMORED WITH USEFULNESS

We have always wanted to be used. How wonderful it is to be useful! But it is so easy to become addicted to usefulness itself that we forget our main business—that of just being his.

It came to me rather suddenly the other day that it is highly dangerous, especially in times of spiritual blessing, to consider as a prime reason of joy the fact that God is using us. As I was thanking God for blessings and opportunities, I was stopped in my prayer, and it seemed as if God were saying to my heart, "Would you love me just the same if all these things were not happening?" I thought very seriously and then prayed that he would give me lips of praise for what he was more than for what he had done. It was glorious to worship him just for himself. This is what he would have us do.

Our own usefulness can become competition for the Savior. We could slip into such human joy because of our own ministry that we could get to the point that we would not let go for anything.

Of course, the simple answer to this is that we must die even to the blessings of revival and personal usefulness. We must remain in the reckoned position of death to everything but Christ in order that he might live and reign supremely. God is obliged, then, to use us and then apply the cross to our lives at that point so that the usefulness itself will not be our downfall.

God is glorified when he can trust a person or people with revival, but when the fact of revival is revered more than God, he must withdraw his power. Let God be praised that he can use us; but let us praise him most of all because he is the Lord and there is none else. Praise the Lord!

LIVING IN EMOTIONAL MANIFESTATIONS

With the first winds of revival there was excitement beyond anything we had ever witnessed. God just clearly manifested himself; and all present, who had open hearts, knew it. But these feelings of excitement will wane simply because this is the nature of our emotional frame. The very same things that happened with the beginning of revival could happen day after day, but the emotions would soon be adjusted, and there would not be the same emotional manifestations. There is a leaning in the human nature to want to keep everything at a high emotional pitch. The tendency is often to deliberately induce emotion when there does not seem to be a feeling of the presence and power of God. This is a dangerous practice.

In fact, if there are qualities of a service that we discover to be inducing emotion for the sake of emotion, these should be deleted. True revival does not depend upon emotional highs for its sustenance.

Sometimes God moves dramatically and there is fire and wind. Other times he moves and there is nothing but a still, small voice. If we are always looking for the fire and wind, we are apt to miss the still, small voice.

Emotional pleasure comes from the worship of God, but it is not the end of worship. God, himself, is the end of worship. If we are not careful we will find ourselves demanding that our emotion "meter" must register a certain high point on the gauge or we will determine that God is not there and revival has vanished. This is exactly what the devil would have us do. If he can snag us on pure emotionalism, he will isolate us from the deepest fellowship with God (which does not depend on emotionalism) and defeat us in the midst of great seasons of blessings. Let us allow God the privilege of acting just like he wants to act, without having to run through our emotions to be "checked out." We must never feel that we have been a part of the glorious scheme of his blessings long enough to be able to "figure him out" in every situation; for if we do, God may choose to do something unique, so drastically different from anything we have

ever known that we will no longer glory in the flesh.
God is ever doing something new. Let us expect it and
not question it. If he would do it quietly or dramatically,
that is his business, not ours. Our emotions are a *gift*
from God. Let us not make them a *god!*

FAILING TO ELEVATE THE PRAYER LIFE

Seasons of blessing demand a growing prayer life. This
is not a luxury; it is a necessity. In the business of revival
it is so easy to forsake the place of prayer for duties
that seem for the moment to be the more pressing. In
times of spiritual visitation there is no more important
work than prayer. And in times like these, prayerlessness
will take its toll immediately. We must learn *intercession*.
Samuel said, "God forbid that I should sin against the
Lord in ceasing to pray for you" (1 Sam. 12:23). Prayer
is warfare as well as spiritual work. It is more than just
a matter of having devotions; it is an absolute necessity
for spiritual survival.

We must learn *resistance* as a part of prayer. The act
of drawing nigh to God is the prelude to resisting the
devil. He is the subtle saboteur in seasons of spiritual
delight and must be dealt with prevailingly.

After the details of the Christian's armour in Ephesians
6, Paul adds, "Praying always with all prayer and suppli-
cation in the Spirit" (v. 18). Paul had previously warned,
"Neither give place to the devil" (Eph. 4:27). I believe
that prayerlessness gives place to the devil. We are to
"Pray without ceasing" (1 Thess. 5:17).

We are to learn to *praise*. How frustrated the devil
gets when he hears the saints praising God. It has become
such a habit around our church that the little preschool
children can be heard "praising the Lord." Not too many
weeks ago a little lad four years old walked up to me

and said, "I've got one thing to say . . . 'PRAISE THE
LORD.'" This was not only cute but was indicative to
me that he had learned a habit that I had not learned
when I was his age. I wish I had. Christ came to give
the *garment of praise* for the *spirit of heaviness*. There
is no habit more uplifting than praise. There is no worship
as reassuring as praise. No wonder the psalmist calls us
to PRAISE THE LORD!

Revival demands growth in prayer. Let us be warned
that more and more we must learn to pray, lest what
God has begun be thwarted by the devil.

LOVING THE BLESSING MORE THAN
THE BLESSER

If our eyes become stationed on any facet in the midst
of spiritual blessing aside from Christ, we are bound for
defeat. God will not allow anything that he gives to remain
in competition with his Son. The face of the life of victory
has many blessings, any one of which could become the
object of our affections. But we must keep in mind that
it is Christ himself, the life of the living God, in us that
is our magnificent obsession. We must never be obsessed
with anything else.

Have you noticed that the nine-fold cluster of the fruit
of the Spirit mentioned in Galatians 5:22-23 is just a
description of Jesus Christ? The verse could be literally
translated, "When the Spirit is in control in you, he will
produce Jesus Christ." Let us then not worship the fruit
of the Spirit but the Spirit of Christ himself.

Likewise, the armor of the Christian is just Jesus Christ.
We are to be dressed up in Jesus Christ. We are literally
to "put on Christ." "For as many of you as have been
baptized into Christ have put on Christ " (Gal. 3:27).

There is no blessing that he gives that is as blessed

as he. Let us not be as eager to *exult* in the blessing as we are to *exalt* the Blesser!

CHARTING THE COURSE OF REVIVAL

"Who knows where the wind blows?" Jesus intimates in John, chapter 3. The Holy Spirit, like the wind, moves where he will and often does not feel obligated to tell us where that is. We are prone to want to know exactly where the Spirit is leading. Like Peter we ask, "What shall this man do?" It is none of our business. We settled that when we laid our lives on the line and claimed the sovereign Spirit of revival. In that moment we gave up having to know where we were going.

After many years in a business, a man might be considered an expert. Not so in the business of the Lord: His need is not for experts, but for disciples. He does not need our help in charting the course of revival. We are to trust him and not be afraid.

"TOUCHING THE ARK"

The lesson of Uzzah in 2 Samuel 6 is an obvious and an unforgettable one. The ark seemed to be tottering, and he simply reached up to steady it or straighten it and was stricken dead. Revival, as did the ark, belongs to God in a unique way, and he will not tolerate man's touch on that which is his.

Though there must be discernment, and though there should be deep sensitivity about the moving of God, under no circumstances are we to put hands on that which is God's and propose to play protector or director. The result may not be death. It may be a life shelved from his service.

That which God has done and is doing is so holy that we dare not touch it even with the best intentions. We must so completely trust him that we can watch him do something that seems absurd and foolish and still be restfully content with the certainty that he knows exactly what he is doing. Though there are times when the "ark of revival" seems to be tottering, we must assume by faith that the God who keeps the universes in order can surely care for this situation within the context of our perfect obedience.

COMPLACENCY AND PRESUMPTION

Among the pitfalls of blessed seasons, perhaps there are none worse than complacency and presumption. These are the terrible twins that are capable of assassinating revival and ending seasons of spiritual delight.

A flippant attitude can be terribly dangerous in revival. The Holy Spirit is grieved when we become complacent regarding sin.

Without care we will find ourselves wondering if God's blessings might continue if thus and thus did not happen. We are then in danger of toying with holy things in the midst of curiosity.

The solution to these problems is simply Jesus Christ, living in us as Lord. Thus, reckoning self dead, we are delivered from the pitfalls along the path as we walk with him.

BEING DRAWN AWAY FROM PRIMARY RESPONSIBILITIES

Revival has come. The fulness of the Spirit has brought a new era of joy and usefulness. There are new demands for help from everywhere. New opportunities clamor for our time.

With the coming of the new, we must keep in mind the existence of the things that were around before revival came. We are still a part of families who need us. We still have responsibilities to people around us. There is no cause so great that we are justified in neglecting primary matters in order to attend to it.

Eli becomes our example and warning in this respect. He was ever busy with the house of the Lord and neglected his own household. His boys turned out to be scoundrels with no respect for their father, his God, or his office. Though he was doubtless a good priest, he is remembered as the man who was too busy to be a good father.

THE NUMBERS RACKET

The peril of counting numbers is greatest in times when God gives more to count and number. If great care is not exercised, we will use numbers to describe what is happening in the midst of the Spirit's visitation and cause others to assume that in them is the greatest measure of revival. The truth is that the real glory of revival can never submit to evaluation by the means of numbers. If we get involved in the "numbers racket," we are apt to get unduly alarmed when God begins his pruning process.

When Gideon's "revival" came, he would have been hard put to explain the numerical result as a glorious success. But after his 32,000 were reduced to 300, those who were left won a resounding victory. I pray that this does not have to happen in your situation for revival to be a reality. It need not have happened to Gideon's army had all of them been *willing* and *prepared!* We must be continually reminded, however, that God does not depend on greatness in numbers to get his job done.

If numbers are referred to as reflecting the magnitude of the work of the Spirit, let it be with thanksgiving to God on every tongue! If we ever use numbers with a "look-what-we-are-doing" attitude, God will withdraw his power and it will become just that—"what *we* are doing."

THE STEREOTYPE SYNDROME

In spiritual experiences we are often given to measuring the experiences of others by our own. This often becomes so intense that we question the validity of the spiritual discoveries of others because they do not correspond to the exact terminology and circumstances of our own. The fulness of the Spirit, and thus the beginning of revival, are different happenings, in different situations, and to different people. Though there will be qualities of sameness, still every situation will have its own individual uniqueness under the Divine hand.

A few months ago I was called to a Free Methodist Church in Spring Arbor, Michigan, to report to the people there the glory of revival in Texas. Can you imagine a Southern Baptist preacher from Texas preaching to a Free Methodist church in Michigan? That has to be revival! I suppose that there was in my mind a tendency to measure that revival in terms of the one raging in our locale. But when I arrived in Spring Arbor, I discovered that the church was different, the people were different, expressions were different, and facets of the revival were different. There was, however, one glorious, gladdening point of sameness . . . the same Holy Spirit was in control, and we glorified God together! A determination to stereotype would have resulted in a lost blessing for me.

God has moved in my heart! He may have done some things for you that he hasn't yet done for me. He may have done some things for me in a manner different from the way he has done them for you. If we will allow God the freedom to do his uniquely beautiful work in each of us, we can praise his name together!

These and many other warnings are in order in seasons of blessings. We do well to look ever to Jesus, not his work nor his blessings. He, not these, is our reward. We are then to "seek . . . God, and his righteousness [which is Jesus]; and all these [other] things shall be added unto you [us]" (Matt. 6:33). Let us claim the gift of discernment in these crisis times of spiritual outpouring. We have Jesus living in us, "In whom are hid all the treasures of wisdom and knowledge" (Col. 2:3). That is enough!

PART III
HOW YOU CAN BE FILLED TODAY

"And when they had prayed, the place was shaken where they were assembled together; and they were all filled with the Holy Ghost, and they spake the word of God with boldness" (Acts 4:31).

That the fulness of the Spirit is God's norm for every Christian today there is no argument. It must be a sad sight for God to see people and churches existing today as if the Holy Spirit had not come. How audacious that we should propose to live and minister without him who was sent to magnify Christ, empower the believer, and teach us about himself . . . the Holy Spirit. How foolish for us to address ourselves to the task of reaching the lost and standing against the adversary without *all* the power of the Holy Spirit in our lives. To have the benefit of all his power is to be filled with the Spirit. To be filled with the Spirit is simply to have chosen to be brought completely under his control, dying to self, and living only to Jesus.

As we begin this most important consideration, there

are two questions which must be asked: (1) Have I been
filled with the Holy Spirit? (2) Am I, right at this moment,
being filled with the Holy Spirit? Both of these questions
are vital. If the answer to the first is affirmative, then
the second is as vital as the first. It is possible to be
filled with the Spirit and then to experience spiritual "leak-
age" due to disobedience.

Victory in the midst of this consideration will wait
on our complete honesty in everything with regard to
our lives. There can be no fabrication here. We must
simply face the imperative, meet the qualifications, and
claim the victory now!

WHY SHOULD WE BE FILLED?

There are several reasons to be given why it is imperative that every believer be filled with the Spirit:

1. It is through the ministry of the Holy Spirit that
the Lord Jesus Christ is exalted. Dare we believe that
by our own puny efforts we can magnify the Son of God?
The Holy Spirit is the Holy Specialist sent to take the
things of Christ and to make them ours. What presumption that we should take upon ourselves the responsibility
of glorifying Christ when the Spirit has come to do it
himself!

2. The Holy Spirit is the Specialist sent to bring men
under the conviction of sin. It is his work and his alone.
Without the Spirit, men can but spark in men lesser motives upon which to come into the kingdom. A work in
the name of evangelism which tends to seek the souls
of men without the thrust of Spirit conviction is a dangerous brand of evangelism indeed. Sad stories may bring
tears; fiery sermons may bring fears; but only the Holy
Spirit brings true conviction unto repentance.

3. There is no other way to overcome the self-life than

through the work of the Holy Spirit constantly applying the meaning of the cross. The Holy Spirit is the great Undertaker who is always taking us to the place of *death to self* that we might be brought to the place of *life in Christ.* Without the constant work of the Holy Spirit filling our lives with himself, we are forever "stirring in the coffin." Our constant consent to his constant application of the deeper meaning of the cross keeps us in the *position of death* that we might constantly know the *power of his Life.*

4. The fulness of the Spirit is the great desire of Christ for each of us. As Jesus prayed for his disciples (and us) in John 17, he prayed, ". . . that they might have my joy fulfilled in themselves" (v. 13). He also said, "And the glory which thou gavest me I have given them" (v. 22). That glory is none other than his indwelling Spirit! Jesus further prayed, "I in them, and thou in me, that they may be made perfect in one" (v. 23).

If a person had not one other aspiration or ambition to be filled with the Spirit than the desire of Jesus, this should be enough!

Knowing that the fulness of the Spirit is necessary for the task of Christian living and ministry, that it is an imperative of inspired Scripture, and that it is the deepest desire of Christ for his very own as evidenced in his prayer . . . how diligently we should seek that FULNESS until we are awash on the flow of those promised rivers (John 7:38).

GETTING ON PRAYING GROUND

Many are ready for the benefits of fulness who are not ready for the process required to be filled. There is no easy way to be filled "in six easy lessons." With the fulness of the Spirit there must come the reckoning of death to the self-life. There is no easy way to come to that.

Getting to the place where we can ask for the fulness of the Spirit involves three areas where God must be satisfied: *refining the motive, approaching Holy God,* and *dealing with sin and sins.* The approach to fulness which does not include these considerations is apt to result in frustration or confusion or both!

I prayed for the fulness of the Spirit in my life for years with the motive for personal power. I have a feeling that I was not alone in such a motive. Being filled with the Spirit brings all the fruit of the Spirit, but none of these are to be the motives for desiring the fulness . . . they are the results. THE HOLY SPIRIT DOES NOT FILL US TO MAKE LIFE ENJOYABLE (though it will be), BUT TO MAKE US EMPLOYABLE!

Everyone wants to be successful but the Holy Spirit will never fill us as long as our motive for seeking him is oriented in success. Watch out, preacher, if you are determined to gear the Holy Spirit down to your promotional schemes! Think twice before you seek to plug into the high-voltage power of the Holy Spirit with your low-voltage appliances for ministerial advancement. Leave your plans and schemes behind when you come to pray for this!

There is one motive, and only one, which is acceptable to God as we come before him with prayer for fulness . . . and that is the LORD JESUS CHRIST HIMSELF. It is he whom we seek. It is ALL OF HIMSELF THAT WE MUST HAVE, *in, over,* and *through* our lives. Jesus told the Father, "And all mine are thine, and thine are mine; *and I am glorified in them*" (John 17:10). The supreme purpose of the fulness, and thus the singular motive for the fulness, is the GLORIFICATION OF THE LORD JESUS CHRIST!

Simon, in Acts 8:18-19, would have bought this power of the Holy Spirit with money. Peter's reply was stern, "Thy money perish with thee, because thou hast thought that the gift of God may be purchased with money. Thou hast neither part nor lot in this matter: for thy heart is not right in the sight of God" (v. 20-21). Simon was not even ready to begin to pray for the fulness because his motives had not been refined. His number is legion today! We need to confess the presence of wrong motives and purely utilitarian attitudes toward the Holy Spirit. Let us allow the fire of God to heat the crucible of our motives until one solitary motive remains . . . the glory of Jesus Christ!

Let us now come to the matter of *approaching Holy God*. The awesomeness of approaching Holy God has dawned on but a few. But for these few has been reserved an insight into his character necessary for the maintaining of a life of holiness pleasing to him. The holiness of God is a concept almost lost in our modern day. It was not so in the Old Testament when the very name of God was without vowel and men feared to say it, lest in mispronouncing it, they be stricken! How different it is today in the average place of business as invectives naming God fill the air.

As we come to approach God on holy business, there is only one avenue by which we can do it. That avenue is the death of Jesus Christ and his resurrection. God cannot look upon sinful man with any toleration except through the death of Jesus on the cross. It is therefore through what Jesus did for us in his suffering and continues to do for us in intercession that we come to the Father. We can come in no other but an humble spirit. We have nothing in our hands with which to bargain for his fulness. We come as undeserving, helpless, hopeless creatures, in the name of Jesus.

Finally, before we come to receive the fulness, we must face the matter of *dealing with sin and sins.* It is death and death alone with which the *sin* problem is cared for. For, while sins involve actions that can be forgiven, sin springs from a nature that cannot be improved. Thus, this sin nature must be placed in the position of death so as to be unproductive of its likeness. Its productive machinery must be incapacitated, disabled, and put out of commission. It is through *sins,* however, that we see the true nature of the self-life as energized by Satan. It is this "covey of sins" that we must flush into the open (every one of them) in order to be emptied for the filling.

Because of his nature and the nature of sin, God cannot tolerate sin in any form. His holiness precludes the possibility that he can put up even with one "little" sin. We must understand how sin affects God. Sin was what sent Jesus to die. Sin was what broke the heart of God and postponed his holy purposes for man. Sin is the insulator which cuts the current between God and man. Sin is the veil through which God cannot be seen. Sin is the short in the system which disallows the full current of God's power from coming through. God's consistency with himself demands that he hate sin. He will not, he cannot take control of any thing or person in which resides the slightest sin.

THEREFORE, IF WE ARE TO BE FILLED WITH THE HOLY SPIRIT, OUR SINS MUST BE CONFESSED UP TO DATE. The promise of the Bible is that "If we confess our sins, he is faithful and just to forgive us our sins, and to cleanse us from all unrighteousness" (1 John 1:9). *Every* sin must be confessed to God. The only thing that keeps you, right now, from being filled with the Holy Spirit is *sin!* It may be the sin of ignorance, or the sin of pride, or the sin of covetousness;

whatever it is that keeps you from God's best is sin! Therefore, it must be dealt with!

But how shall we deal with the problem of sin? The
only answer is . . . *straightforwardly!* We will deal with
the sin nature as the Holy Spirit fills us. What stands
in the way of filling right now is unforgiven sins. Bertha
Smith, one of God's mightiest Spirit-filled soldiers, suggests that we write our sins out on a sheet of paper.
This will help us to honestly face them. The name of
the sin should be faced. Everything in the heart and life
that is unholy should be included on the list. *Nothing*
should be left out. When you have named every word,
deed, thought, and disposition that is unholy, then ask
God to turn the lights on in your heart and show you
all the things you missed! He will heartily oblige. When
you have listed all you can think of and all God has
reminded you of, then have a long look at the entire
list and observe what you look like to Holy God! Have
you ever seen anything as repulsive in all your life?

Now there is value in writing down your sins. You
will have a tendency not to take them seriously until
you see their true nature as being against God. You will
come to hate sin as he hates sin if you will face its nature.

Every revival about which I have read was initiated
by honesty in prayer and confession of sin. This is without
exception. People must face their sins if the Holy Spirit
is to have control. As people have become honest, even
the "smallest" of sins loom large as the Holy Spirit brings
conviction.

A missionary returned his seminary diploma over dishonesty regarding a cafeteria bill while in the seminary
years before.

Seminary students fabricated their parallel reading reports and had to confess.

College students in recent meetings confessed to dishonesty over tests and lessons and made things straight with professors.

A woman in another state was moved to publicly confess a sin committed twelve years previously which involved a small sum of money.

A preacher had to confess the theft of a small comb and brush set taken when he was a junior boy.

My associate confessed to taking out a lay-away item without paying for it completely years ago in a store where he worked. (God led him back to the town where this happened, and he had the glad privilege of paying it back!)

A prominent man of means confessed an unpaid debt of thirty years standing, figured the going rate of interest for thirty years, added it up, and paid the debt in full!

If you are having trouble in listing your sins, the following may help. This is the text of a little tract whose author is unknown. Reading it before listing your sins will be of (ugh!) help.

"The following are some of the features and manifestations of the self-life. The Holy Spirit alone can interpret and apply this to your individual case. As you read, examine yourself in the very presence of God. Are you ever conscious of:

"A secret sense of pride . . . an exalted feeling, in view of your success or position; because of your good training or appearance; because of your natural gifts and abilities? An important, independent spirit?

"Love of human praise; a secret fondness to be noticed; love of supremacy, drawing attention to self in conversation; a swelling out of self when you have had a free time in speaking or praying?

"The stirrings of anger or impatience, which, worst of all, you call nervousness or holy indignation; a touchy, sensitive spirit; a disposition to resent and retaliate when disapproved of or contradicted; a desire to throw sharp, heated flings at another?

"Self-will; a stubborn, unteachable spirit; an arguing, talkative spirit; harsh, sarcastic expression; an un-yielding, headstrong disposition; a driving, commanding spirit; a disposition to criticize and pick flaws when set aside and unnoticed; a peevish, fretful spirit; a disposition that loves to be coaxed and humored?

"Carnal fear; a man-fearing spirit; a shrinking from reproach and duty; reasoning around your cross; a shrinking from doing your whole duty by those of wealth or position; a fearfulness that someone will offend and drive some prominent person away; a compromising spirit?

"A jealous disposition; a secret spirit of envy shut up in your heart; an unpleasant sensation in view of the great prosperity and success of another; a disposition to speak of the faults and failings, rather than the gifts and virtues of those more talented and appreciated than yourself?

"A dishonest, deceitful disposition; the evading and covering of the truth; the covering up of your real faults; leaving a better impression of yourself than is strictly true; false humility; exaggeration; straining the truth?

"Unbelief; a spirit of discouragement in times of pressure and opposition; lack of quietness and confidence in God; lack of faith and trust in God; a disposition

to worry and complain in the midst of pain,
poverty, or at the dispensations of Divine
Providence; an overanxious feeling whether
everything will come out all right?
"Formality and deadness; lack of concern for lost souls;
dryness and indifference; lack of power with God?
"Selfishness, love of ease; love of money?

"These are some of the traits which generally indicate
a carnal heart. By prayer, hold your heart open to the
searchlight of God, until you see the groundwork thereof.
'Search me, O God, and know my heart: try me, and
know my thoughts: and see if there be any wicked way
in me' (Ps. 139:23-24).

"The Holy Ghost will enable you, by confession and
faith, to bring your 'self-life' to the death. Do not patch
over, but go to the bottom. It alone will pay.

"Oh, to be saved from myself, dear Lord,
    Oh, to be lost in Thee;
Oh, that it might be no more I,
    But Christ that lives in me.

'Create in me a clean heart, O God; and renew a right
spirit within me' " (Ps. 51:10).

After you have looked over that list and your confession
has been made to God, you can mark out all those that
were just against God. There will be others that were
against people. Some of these can only be completely
settled when you have made restitution or satisfaction.
It may take a long distance phone call or a letter. It
may take a drive across town. Whatever you have to
do to put yourself on praying ground will be worth it!
The devil will try to tell you how foolish all this is. He
will say, "After all, doesn't God forgive sins? Why involve

others in your confession?" You see, the devil knows all too well that if you get all your sins settled, you are going to be filled, and this will be *for him* the worst day in your life.

Once we get on praying ground by getting the motive right, approaching God through the death of Jesus, and settling the problems of our sins, we are then ready to do business with Holy God regarding the Holy Spirit's fulness.

PRAYING THROUGH TO VICTORY

With sins confessed we are then ready to *choose the Lord's will in advance in every situation* which concerns us and ours. In this act of choosing his will we are yielding not only all we know of ourselves to all that we know of him but what we do not know as well. We are signing a contract so trustfully that we do not bother to read the print. This is a deliberate choice against ourselves in preference to him. To choose him is to choose against self. The nature of this choice is illustrated by an old Methodist covenant of consecration:

> I am no longer my own, but Thine. Put me to what
> Thou wilt; rank me with whom Thou wilt; put me
> to doing; put me to suffering; let me be employed
> by Thee or laid aside for Thee; exalted for Thee
> or brought low for Thee; let me be full; let
> me be empty; let me have all things; let
> me have nothing; I freely and heartily
> yield all things to thy pleasure and
> disposal.

We are then ready for the next step—*choosing the position of death to self.* We are not to stop with choosing against ourselves. We must make the choice of death to

self. Jesus said, "If any man will come after me, let him
deny himself, and take up his cross daily, and follow
me" (Luke 9:23). We are to choose death to our plans,
ambitions, tastes, friends, securities, wealth, future, reputation, and everything else in order that we might live
unto Christ.

Oh, wonderful is the fact of his death for us; but even
more wonderful is the fact of ours *with* him! We do not
have to accomplish it; it has already been done. We need
only to choose the position and reckon it so.

> There's a little word that the Lord has given,
>   For our help in the hour of need . . .
> Let us *reckon* ourselves to be dead to sin,
>   To be dead to sin indeed.

> There's another word that the Lord has given . . .
>   In the very same verse we read:
> Let us *reckon* our selves as alive in him,
>   As alive and alive indeed.

> Let us *reckon!* RECKON! RECKON!
>   RECKON rather than feel!
> Let us be true to the reckoning,
>   And God will make it real.[20]

"If it die" is a wonderful supposition! Jesus was talking
about himself in John 12:24. He was also talking about
us. If we die to our own identity, we then are free to
live to him. Are you ready to deliberately choose the
position of death to that old self so that he might be
your new self? Then do it right now.

Next, we are ready with an act of the will to *enthrone
Jesus Christ in our lives*. He has wanted that position in
our lives all along and has been waiting on our *wills.*

He will never break our will, but when we choose to synchronize our wills with his, he does what he has always wanted to do . . . takes control of our lives. The very moment we invite him with cleansed hearts to take the throne of our lives, he does so!

Finally, we are to simply *appropriate, accept, believe,* and *thank him* that he begins, as the first official act of his reign in our hearts, to fill us with the Holy Spirit. At the very moment he takes the throne, the position in which he is glorified, he fills us with his Spirit. Just as it was in history so it will be in our lives. "The Holy Ghost was *not yet* given; because that Jesus was *not yet* glorified" (John 7:39). The very moment that Jesus was glorified in heaven, the Holy Spirit was poured out upon the earth. If Jesus is *not yet* glorified in your life and mine as Lord, we are confronted with the other *"not yet"* regarding the fulness. But . . . if we have crowned Jesus as Lord, we may be assured, on the basis of the Scripture, that HE IS FILLING US WITH HIS SPIRIT!

> Are you waiting for his Spirit,
>   And the fulness of his power?
> Yield yourself in full surrender
>   And he'll come this very hour.
> Like the light that flows from heaven,
>   Like the streams that flow so free,
> God is giving, always giving,
>   All the hindrance is with thee.[21]

It is vital that we appropriate the fulness in the same manner that we received salvation . . . by faith. Having met his condition, we simply believe.

My friend, there is a new life awaiting you right now. You need not wait a moment longer. God has done all he is going to do. He has done all he *needs* to do! The

next move is up to you. Would you choose to go from
here back to a life of struggle and futile toil? You need
not! You dare not! God's desire to enthrone Christ in
your life and fill you with his blessed Spirit is infinitely
greater than your desire could ever be. But he is waiting
on you.

Would you just now look back over the points of this
chapter and ponder them for a moment:

Are you on praying ground? . . . .
   having your motive refined? . . . .
      approaching God through Jesus' name? . . . ,
         confessing your sins up to date and making
           restitution?

Will you now choose his will in advance in every
situation?

Will you deliberately choose the position of death for
yourself?

Will you with an act of your will enthrone Christ in
your life?

Will you appropriate the fulness of the Spirit by faith?

If you can answer these in the affirmative you are ready
to pray. Make this your prayer:

Lord, I have confessed and settled every sin of which
you have convicted me.

I now choose your will in advance in every situation
in direct opposition to and rejection of myself.

I choose the position of death to myself.

LORD JESUS, I ENTHRONE YOU AS SOVER-
EIGN LORD IN MY LIFE RIGHT NOW.

Now, that you are Lord, I thank you that I can receive
right at this moment the fulness of the Holy Spirit.

I thank you, Holy Spirit, that you have been in my
heart ever since I have been born again. Now I thank

you that you are filling my life and magnifying Christ in me!

In Jesus name . . . . amen!

If you have honestly prayed in this manner, God has promised to meet your faith with his promise fulfilled. Remember, it is continuous appropriation of a continuous supply from Jesus. It is a moment-by-moment faith in a moment-by-moment Savior, for a moment-by-moment cleansing, and a moment-by-moment filling. It is a moment-by-moment dying to self that we might know his moment-by-moment life. This is the manner in which we can live in constant victory.

Thus we discover . . .

THE KEY TO TRIUMPHANT LIVING! . . .

CHRIST RESIDING IN THE HUMAN LIFE . . .

REIGNING OVER THE HUMAN LIFE . . .

AND

RELEASED THROUGH THE HUMAN LIFE . . .

BY THE HOLY SPIRIT!

"AND OUT OF YOUR INNER MAN WILL FLOW . . .

RIVERS OF LIVING WATER!"

May this continuing experience be yours!

NOTES

CHAPTER 1

1. Mrs. Charles E. Cowman, *Streams in the Desert* (Published by Mrs. Charles E. Cowman, 1925), p. 155.
2. Loc. cit.

CHAPTER 3

3. McCall Barbour, *When Did You Die?* (Barbour Publishing, Inc.), p. 12.
4. McCall Barbour, *How to Die Daily* (Barbour Publishing, Inc.), p. 23.
5. L. E. Maxwell, *Born Crucified* (Chicago: Moody Press), p. 63.

CHAPTER 5

6. Figure by Ralph Neighbour, Jr.
7. *Ibid.*
8. *Ibid.*
9. *Ibid.*
10. *Ibid.*

CHAPTER 6

11. McCall Barbour, *How to Die Daily* (Barbour Publishing, Inc.), p. 9.

CHAPTER 10

12. John R. Rice, *The Power of Pentecost* (Murfreesboro, Tenn.: Sword of the Lord Publishers), p. 392.
13. V. Raymond Edman, *They Found the Secret* (Grand Rapids: Zondervan Publishing House) p. 44-49.
14. Rice, *op. cit.,* p. 404.
15. Rice, *op. cit.,* p. 408.

16. Charles Trumbull, *Victory in Christ* (Fort Washington, Pa.: Christian Literature Crusade, Inc., 1970), pp. 9-14.
17. Lindley Baldwin, *March of Faith* (Minneapolis, Minn.: Bethany Fellowship, Inc. 1969), p. 46.

CHAPTER 16

18. *Not I But Christ,* tract
19. L. E. Maxwell, *Abandoned to Christ* (Grand Rapids: Wm. B. Eerdmans Publishing Co.), p. 16.
20. McCall Barbour, *When Did You Die?* (Barbour Publishing, Inc.), p. 15.
21. A. B. Simpson, *Songs of the Spirit* (Harrisburg, Pa.: Christian Publications, Inc.), p. 53.

A Book List on Christian Growth
Recommended by Jack R. Taylor

BRIGHT, BILL. *How to Walk in the Spirit.*

CHAMBERS, OSWALD. *My Utmost for His Highest.* New York: Dodd, Mead & Company.

EDMAN, V. RAYMOND. *They Found the Secret.* Grand Rapids: Zondervan Publishing House.

GRUBB, NORMAN. *The Liberating Secret.* Fort Washington, Pennsylvania: Christian Literature Crusade, Inc., 1962.

———. "The Key to Everything" (booklet)

HUEGEL, F. J. *Bone of His Bone.* Grand Rapids: Zondervan Publishing House, 1949.

HUNTER, JOHN. *Knowing God's Secrets.* Grand Rapids: Zondervan Publishing House.

———. *Let Us Go on to Maturity.* Grand Rapids: Zondervan Publishing House, 1968.

———. *Limiting God.* Grand Rapids: Zondervan Publishing House.

LETGERS, L. L. *The Simplicity of the Spirit-Filled Life.*

McCONKEY, JAMES H. *The Three-Fold Secret of the Holy Spirit.* Chicago: Moody Press, 1897.

———. *The Surrendered Life.*

———. *The Way of Victory.*

MEYER, F. B. *The Christ-Life for the Self Life.* Chicago: Moody Press.

MURRAY, ANDREW. *Abide in Christ.* Fort Washington, Pennsylvania: Christian Literature Crusade, Inc., 1963-1968.

NEE, WATCHMAN. *The Normal Christian Life.* Fort Washington, Pennsylvania: Christian Literature Crusade, Inc., 1961-1963.

———. *Sit, Walk, and Stand.* Fort Washington, Pennsylvania: Christian Literature Crusade, Inc., 1964.

PAXSON, RUTH. *Rivers of Living Waters.*

_____. *Life on the Highest Plane.* Chicago: Moody Press, 1928.

PRICE, WALTER. *Channels of Power.*

REDPATH, ALAN. *Victorious Christian Living.* Old Tappan, New Jersey: Fleming H. Revell Company, 1955.

SIMPSON, A. B. "Himself" (tract)

SMITH, BERTHA. *Go Home and Tell.* Nashville: Broadman, 1965.

SMITH, HANNAH W. *Christian's Secret of a Happy Life.* New York: Grosset & Dunlap, 1958.

_____. *God of All Comfort.*

_____. *Everyday Religion.* Chicago: Moody Press.

STAFORD, MILES. *Green Letters of Principles of Spiritual Growth.*

_____. *Red Letters.*

_____. *Principles of Position.*

_____. *The Reckoning That Counts.*

_____. *Abide Above.*

THOMAS, IAN. *The Saving Life of Christ.* Grand Rapids: Zondervan Publishing House, 1961.

_____. The Mystery of Godliness. Grand Rapids: Zondervan Publishing House, 1964.

TRUMBULL, CHARLES. *Victory in Christ.* Fort Washington, Pennsylvania: Christian Literature Crusade, Inc., 1970.

TRYON, DAVID. "But How . . ." (booklet)

UNKNOWN CHRISTIAN. *How to Live the Victorious Christian Life.* Grand Rapids: Zondervan Publishing House.

_____. *The Kneeling Christian.* Grand Rapids: Zondervan Publishing House.